45 87   D0353365

Hertfordshire
COUNTY COUNCIL
Community Information

Frances Lincoln Limited
4 Torriano Mews
Torriano Avenue
London NW5 2RZ
www.franceslincoln.com

A catalogue record for this book is available from the British Library.

978-0-7112-3120-7

Printed and bound in China

3 4 5 6 7 8 9

FOR CHAR AND LUX

CONTENTS

WELCOME

It was the summer of 1989, I'd just witnessed the American Greg LeMond win the Tour de France and by this point my life was totally consumed by cycling. I'd bought a nice Raleigh racing bike the summer before and been out on a few rides but nothing serious. Seeing LeMond beat Laurent Fignon by just eight seconds, after three weeks of edge-of-the-seat racing lit a fire in my heart that still burns as strong today. The following week I took my Ordnance Survey maps to my uncle's house and begged him to show me where the toughest local hills were. Being brought up on the border of Nottinghamshire and Lincolnshire I wasn't exactly in the heart of hill climbing country but hoped there was one killer hill hidden out there. My uncle, my original cycling mentor, knew exactly what I sought and pointed me in the direction of Terrace Hill (No. 29). The next weekend, my friend and I set off to find our mecca. We conquered the climb and thoroughly satisfied we stopped at the top for lunch. A year later, I won my first race up the very same road, I was totally hooked on climbing.

Since the invention of the bicycle, overcoming the pull of gravity has been the simplest and purest cycling challenge. Long before scientific training methods, heart rate monitors and power meters were invented the way to get fit was to ride up hills, lots of them. Having ridden up countless hills over the years and having indulged in many a mad pilgrimage in search of a yet steeper stretch of tarmac I thought it was time there was a pocket guide to these great roads. Britain doesn't have the mountain ranges other countries can boast, but what it does have are plenty of little killer climbs, hidden in towns or crossing windswept moors and they pack in as much character as an alpine pass.

Compiled here isn't merely a list of the 100 steepest roads, nor is it simply a list of the 100 highest passes. My starting point was ascents that are famous as hill-climb courses. Traditionally held at the end of the racing season, hill climbs are short and brutal events. They test riders like no other race can, and the same fabled courses have been used for generations. It is hill climbing that cemented my passion for cycling. Although I wasn't a winner I could compete with the best and what I lacked in ability I made up for in preparation, I studied each hill before the event so I knew it inside out. My favorite always was, and still is, Riber in Matlock, Derbyshire (No. 32). After it veers off the main road it's like a bonsai Alpine pass, cramming in a mountain's ▶▶

worth of climbing in under 500 metres, forever switching back and forth and just so steep. After charting Britain's best-known hill-climb courses, I headed to the roads that are famously steep or challenging, not just in cycling circles but among anyone with knowledge of the geography of the nation's most jagged regions.

Once I had drawn up a long list of climbs I set certain criteria for all inclusions and also solid reasons for any notable exclusions, such as the road up to the radar station on Great Dunn Fell. The highest paved road in the UK it may be but technically it's a private road so I decided it didn't quite fit the bill. Another common consideration came due to the fact that roads that go up one side of a hill invariably come down the other side. It's often a hard choice to opt for one ascent over the other, so I had to make a judgment call based not purely on gradient and length but on the overall cycling experience. This cycling experience can be uniquely personal, how one climb feels to one person maybe totally different to how it feels to another. There are some hills I could have ridden all day but others, which on paper look very similar, had me begging for mercy, Chapel Fell (No. 62) being one such example. I hated every second

of it, and it ground me down like no other hill I'd visited. Some hills can differ greatly depending on the context in which they are ridden. Michaelgate in Lincoln (No. 28) is perfectly manageable on a club run, but when I rode it as part of the Lincoln Grand Prix it was an entirely different prospect.

So here's my list of 100 and like any list I expect and hope it will be the cause for lively conversation. Is your local leg-breaker included? Are you outraged by the exclusion of your favorite training hill? Or just plain baffled at some rather weak looking inclusions. I set myself a limit of 100 ascents and ensured there was a geographical spread so as not to favour one region too heavily. Stripped down to its basics, this book is simply a guide to point you in the direction of amazing roads. While I hope that club rooms and forums will be filled with debate and maybe even anger about the list, more importantly I am hoping that cyclists of all abilities, unaware of what lies both on their doorstep and further afield, will venture out and conquer the hills for themselves. These roads are the cyclists' theaters, our stadia, they are beautiful, challenging, provide us with an immense sense of achievement and to top all that they are great fun to ride.

LEGEND

UNDERSTANDING THE FACTFILES AND RATINGS

LOCATIONS

You will be able to locate each hill from the small maps, simply, **S** marks the start and **F** marks the finish. I would suggest you invest in either Ordnance Survey maps or a GPS system to help plan your routes in more detail. The grid reference in the factfile locates the summit of each climb and in brackets is the relevant **OS Landranger** map. The graphic at the start of each chapter will show you where the hills lie in the context of each region.

TIMINGS

Each factfile includes the approximate time needed to ride each hill. Timed over the distance marked, this is how long it took me to complete each climb at a reasonable, but comfortable pace. Since I rode in all weathers from blizzards to baking heat, I have adjusted the times slightly to accommodate for the adverse conditions I faced on the day. The times could be used as a target but are really just intended as a rough guide.

FACTFILE

WHERE Leave the A646 north of Sowerby Bridge and turn onto Luddenden Lane. Continue north until the road forks and take the right fork onto High Street. Next take the second right onto Halifax Lane and begin.

GRID REF SE 053 257 (**OS**104)

LENGTH 1630m

HEIGHT GAIN 185m

APPROX CLIMB TIME 9mins

RATINGS

The climbs are rated from **1/10** to **10/10** within the context of the book. The rating is an amalgamation of gradient, length, the likely hostility of the riding conditions and the condition of the surface. All the climbs are tough, therefore **1/10** equals 'hard', and **10/10** equals 'it's all you can do to keep your bike moving'. Some will suit you more than others, the saying 'horses for courses' applies, but all the **10/10** climbs will test any rider.

MAP KEY

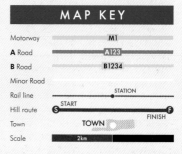

Motorway	M1
A Road	A123
B Road	B1234
Minor Road	
Rail line	STATION
Hill route	START S ——— F FINISH
Town	TOWN
Scale	2km

LONGEST AND STEEPEST

How do our toughest and steepest climbs compare to those around the world? Obviously we are never going to be able to replicate the giants of the Tour de France, we just don't have the geography. Mountains such as the Alpe d'Huez, famous for the 21 hairpins it packs into its 13.8 kilometres, or the fearsome Mont Ventoux, the 'Giant of Provence'. This beast boasts three grueling routes to the top, all offering over 20 kilometres of climbing. Mighty as these are even they are dwarfed by the world's longest climbs such as the 45-kilometre climb up Mount Evans in Colorado, USA. Or the huge ascent up the Mount Haleakala on Maui. Here you ride from sea level to over 3050 metres in 61 kilometres of relentless toil, from the tropical coast to the snow capped peak in one continuous accent.

Baldwin Street, Dunedin

Clearly unable to compete on a grand scale, can we boast the world's steepest road here in the UK? Well, officially no, the *Guinness Book of Records* bestows that honor on Baldwin Street in Dunedin, New Zealand. Having visited this street, alas without a bicycle, I can vouch for its maddening gradient. I fully intended on driving up it in our camper van but as we hit the ramp and debris on the dashboard fell back in my face I chickened out and chose to experience it on foot. The perversity of Baldwin Street had its origins in London, because it was here on the other side of the world that the town's grid system was devised, of course with no consideration of terrain or gradient. Listed as 35%, this doesn't match the claimed 40% of Ffordd Penllech in Harlech. What sets it apart is that from the moment it kicks up its gradient is an all but uniform and remorseless 35% from bottom to top.

Overlooked by Guinness, perhaps the true claim to the title of the steepest road lies in Pittsburgh, USA. Canton Street is measured at an eye watering 37% but again it's not as long as Baldwin Street. Following this you have Fargo Street in Los Angeles at 32% and the mighty Filbert Street in San Francisco at 31.5%. These however are streets, the steepest sealed road must surely be the Via Scanuppia in Besenello, Italy. The road up to the Malga Palazzo is rated at an impossible 45%! I'd love to give it a try, and you can witness some attempts on YouTube. Could this be the ultimate steep road to conquer on two wheels?

GLOSSARY

BELGIAN CLIMBS

There are no mountains in Belgium but what they do have are vicious, rugged, cobbled climbs. Races such as Het Volk and the Tour of Flanders test the limits of the riders' strength and equally skill up these brutal and uneven cobbles. Names such as the Muur-Kapelmuur, the Kemmelberg, Oude Kwaremont and the Molenburg have been creating legends and destroying reputations for generations.

CHRIS BOARDMAN

One of our nation's most decorated cyclists, he dominated the domestic time trial scene and won four consecutive National Hill-Climb Championships. After taking gold in the 4km pursuit at the 1992 Olympics he turned professional and went on to win the prologue (opening time trial) of the Tour de France three times.

CYCLING TIME TRIALS

The majority of Hill-Climbs in the UK are run under CTT rules, the governing body for road time trials.

CC

The abbreviation used for a cycling club, i.e. Norwood Paragon CC.

GRADIENTS

Gradients are marked on signs in one of two ways. For example either as 1-in-4, or for the same gradient, 25%. Basically in the case of 1-in-4 for every 4 metres travelled horizontally you will travel 1 metre vertically.

GREG LEMOND

Winner of the Tour de France three times, in 1986, 1989 and 1990. He famously came back from a life threatening hunting accident to win the race by just 8 seconds in 1989 in the greatest finish the race has ever seen.

HILL-CLIMB

A Hill-Climb is simply a race up a designated hill/course where the riders are set off at minute intervals and the winner is the rider recording the quickest time. Running from late September until the end of October the season culminates with the National Hill-Climb Championship. Generally held on the last full weekend in the month the event attracts the countrys' best climbers aiming to add their name to the list of winners going back to 1944. Hill-Climbs always attract a crowd and those such as the Catford CC and Bec CC Hill-Climbs have an atmosphere to match that found on the side of any mountain stage in the Tour de France.

HILL-CLIMB COURSES

Many of the roads listed in the book are official courses. I have mapped the majority of hills from base to summit, however a hill climb course usually starts partially up the slope so the rider starts on a steep incline.

LINCOLN GRAND PRIX

The Lincoln GP is one of the UK's cycling monuments, a race that all riders would love to win. What gives it its unique character and endears it to both riders and the public alike is the cobbled climb of Michaelgate. Whilst the Lincoln GP is now entering its 55th year, many other great races mentioned in this book such as the Archer GP and the Tour of the Peak have since bitten the dust.

MALCOLM ELLIOTT

One of Britain's cycling greats and still racing today, Malcolm was a professional cyclist between 1984 and 1997. His victories include two Commonwealth gold medals, the sprinters points jersey and two stages of the Tour of Spain.

MILK RACE

From 1960 to 1993 (the Kellogg's Tour was also run from 1987 to 1993) the Tour of Britain was know as the Milk Race due to its sponsorship by the Milk Marketing Board. It became a household name and is still to this day the one cycling event that the majority of Britons have heard of.

TOUR DE FRANCE

The world's greatest and toughest bike race. Held every July, only the world's finest cyclists can dream of riding let alone winning. First run in 1903 its iconic leader's yellow jersey is the most recognised symbol of cycle sport.

TOUR OF BRITAIN

A cycling tour of Britain has existed in one form or another almost every year since 1945. Its most famous incarnation was the Milk Race and currently it is known as the Tour of Britain again.

CYCLO-SPORTIVES

Cyclo-Sportive or simply Sportive rides are not races but timed events run over a testing course and to succeed is to complete the distance. Many in Europe trace epic stages of famous races over mountains and cobbles. Those in the UK can be equally tough such as the 'Fred Whitton' in the Lake District or the 'Dave Lloyd Mega Challenge' in north Wales.

THE HILL CLIMBER

So what makes a great climber? To begin with you need the one key ingredient all top athletes have: that's natural ability. Often referred to as 'class', natural ability is what you are born with, the strength of your heart, the size of your lungs. These things are written in your genes.

You require from your body the ultimate power-to-weight ratio. You need to be light, yet strong, simply the more power you can generate per kilogram of body mass the better you'll ride up hills. On shorter climbs, strong, heavy riders can keep up with the lightweights, but as soon as they reach a long mountain they drop like a brick.

The greatest climbers of all time were Federico Bahamontes and Lucien Van Impe. They both won the King of the Mountains in the Tour de France six times, Bahamontes earning the nickname the Eagle of Toledo for the way he soared away from the opposition. More recent King of the Mountains winners have been tainted by drugs though. The Frenchman Richard Virenque holds the record with seven polka dot jerseys, but having been caught using banned substances they are somewhat tarnished.

As climbing is cycling's toughest discipline, where reputations are made, it has become the one prize that riders have been prepared to risk everything for, including their lives, and cheat to win.

Britain's most decorated climber is the Scot Robert Millar. To this day, he's the only Briton to win the King of the Mountains at the Tour de France. He took the famous polka dot jersey in 1984 and also won the mountains jersey at the 1987 Giro d'Italia.

Domestically, however, our climbers are judged by their performance in the National Hill-Climb Championship. To win this highly specialised event, usually held up a short sharp incline, you need to be an excellent athlete but not essentially a pure lightweight. The race does favour those tipping the scales under 60 kilogrammes, but riders with a massive power output have also triumphed despite a weight disadvantage. The rider with more national titles than anyone else was Granville Sydney. He took the first of his six titles in 1963 up Peaslows (No. 37) and 10 years later his last victory up Dover's Hill (No. 13).

Following in his footsteps with five wins apiece are Stuart Dangerfield and lightweight hill-climbing specialist Jim Henderson. Leading those with four titles is Chris Boardman. Boardman went on to ride the Tour de France five times, but the excellence he displayed on our short UK climbs didn't translate to the high mountains. Just as there's more than one type of climb, there's also more than one type of climber.

BEFORE YOU BEGIN

TAKE CARE AND ENJOY YOURSELF

CHECK YOUR **BIKE**, CHECK YOUR **BODY**, AND ALWAYS WEAR A **HELMET**.

Many of the roads in this book cross the wildest and most inhospitable parts of the nation. You'll often find yourself in open and exposed country so have a good look at the weather forecast before you head out. Although far from impossible most of the climbs require a good level of fitness so only attempt the really tough ones if you are confident of your ability. Remember that what goes up at 1-in-4 is also likely to come down at 1-in-4 so check your brakes and most of all have fun.

SOUTH-WEST

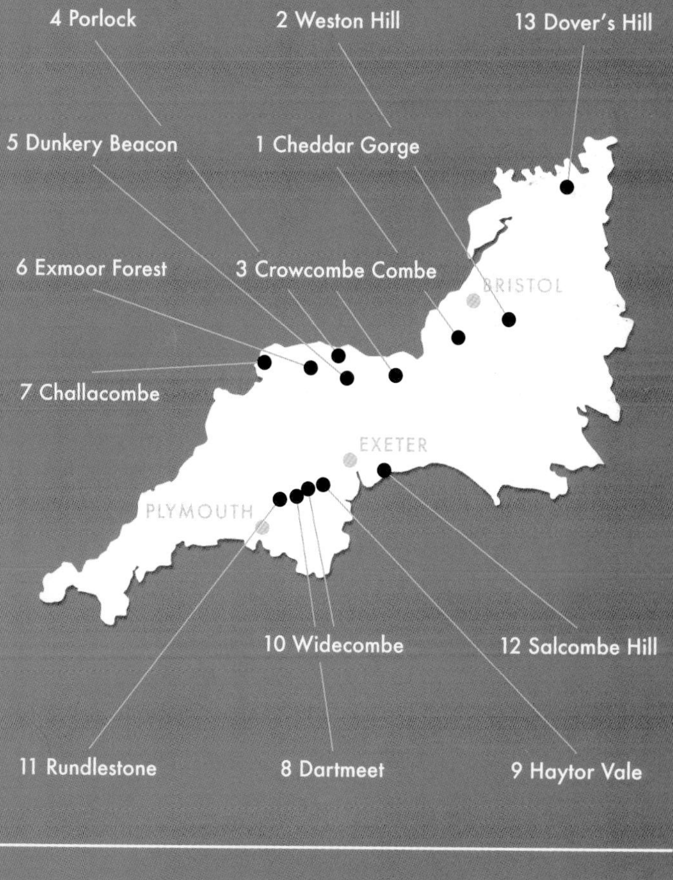

4 Porlock

2 Weston Hill

13 Dover's Hill

5 Dunkery Beacon

1 Cheddar Gorge

6 Exmoor Forest

3 Crowcombe Combe

BRISTOL

7 Challacombe

EXETER

10 Widecombe

12 Salcombe Hill

PLYMOUTH

11 Rundlestone

8 Dartmeet

9 Haytor Vale

1 CHEDDAR GORGE

CHEDDAR, SOMERSET

Cut deep into the Mendip Hills lies Cheddar Gorge, a natural phenomenon that makes a stunning setting to climb through. Start from a little plateau alongside a pond, past the gift shops and the asphalt kicks up steep through large car parks on either side of the road. The surface is excellent and the road is wide and, like Box Hill in Surrey, you will always find cyclists on its slopes as it offers a tough but not overwhelming challenge to riders of all abilities. With the gorge's rock faces towering around you, you'll soon reach the hardest 16% section. A couple of sweeping bends and you're through the worst; as the sides of the gorge diminish, so does the severity of the slope. This climb can flatter the rider like no other – the higher you climb the easier it gets and the faster you ride. With each revolution you'll gain momentum, click up through the gears and finish with a flourish as the road flattens on the hilltop.

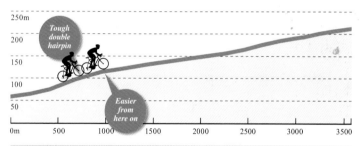

Tough double hairpin

Easier from here on

FACTFILE

WHERE Leave the A371 Church Street and turn onto the B3135 Union Street. This turns into Cliff Street and then The Cliffs which leads you to the base just past Cox's Cave.

GRID REF ST 485 535 (OS182)	
LENGTH 3540m	
HEIGHT GAIN 150m	
APPROX CLIMB TIME 13mins	

2 WESTON HILL

WESTON, BATH

Landsdown Lane leaves Weston in the north-west corner of Bath and heads up the ridge overlooking the city below. Bath is packed full with steep roads much like its neighbour Bristol, which is great if you like climbing but must be tough on those residents who'd rather have an easier commute to work. With hardly a stretch of flat you don't have to look far for a decent urban challenge, but to escape the city, Weston Hill is the route to take. Begin from the roundabout at the head of Weston High Street and pick your way along the rough surface through houses. Soon enough you will have left the urban surroundings behind as you progress up the ridge. The wide road, smoother now on its upper slopes, meanders as it delivers you to its 20% section. Short and sweet, the road banks left, ramps up then kinks right, levelling out 100 metres before the junction with Landsdown Road.

FACTFILE

WHERE From the centre of Bath head west on Weston Road. Follow the road as it turns into Weston Lane, then Crown Road and finally High Street to begin the climb up Lansdown Lane from the roundabout.

GRID REF ST 728 684 (**OS**172)

LENGTH 1870m

HEIGHT GAIN 165m

APPROX CLIMB TIME 8mins

3 CROWCOMBE COMBE

CROWCOMBE, SOMERSET

Running in an almost dead straight line from the base to the summit of the Quantock Hills lies the tough climb out of Crowcombe. For the perfect hill to race up – one that will really suit the true climbers – look no further. This short, quiet stretch of road has plenty of 25% gradient, ample parking at its base and natural banks for spectators. It's hard from the very start; leave the village and veer left, through the trees, past the 1-in-4 sign where the road levels slightly adjacent to an escape lane for runaway vehicles. The super-smooth road heads up straight and steep, first at 20%, then for a short while 25% before easing back to 20% and bending gently to the right. Near the summit comes the hardest section, a left-hand bend ushering in 30 metres of leg-breaking 25% before finally levelling as you enter woods and rumble, stars in your eyes, across a cattle grid to finish.

FACTFILE

WHERE Heading north leave the A358 just past Flaxpool and turn into Crowcombe. Ride to the the centre of the village and turn east opposite the car park and head upwards.

GRID REF ST 149 374 (OS181)	
LENGTH 1270m	
HEIGHT GAIN 188m	
APPROX CLIMB TIME 8.5mins	

4 PORLOCK

PORLOCK, SOMERSET

As the road climbs out of Porlock, west to Lynmouth, you see the warning sign: Gradient 1-in-4. Uphill! This isn't for the faint-hearted. Pass the sign, easing left and there in front of you, rising like a skyscraper, the fearsome 1-in-4 right-hand bend. Wrench your bike into the darkness under the trees and grind along more 1-in-4 to the next bend, this time a left-hander and steeper, nigh on vertical at its apex, where you are forced to the centre of the road in order to keep momentum. Bank right, now just 1-in-5, the air filled with the stench of burning clutches from vehicles as they struggle past. A false summit marks the end of the back-breaking lower slopes and now a much more manageable gradient takes you further up the ridge. Another brow in the road and you're at the top. Or are you? No, there's still one final hard stretch to go before you can stop to admire the view of the coast in the distance below.

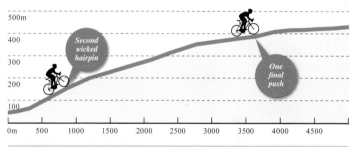

Second wicked hairpin

One final push

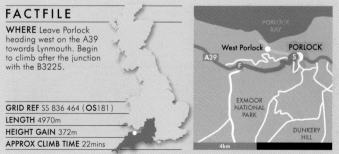

FACTFILE

WHERE Leave Porlock heading west on the A39 towards Lynmouth. Begin to climb after the junction with the B3225.

PORLOCK BAY

West Porlock   **PORLOCK**

A39

EXMOOR NATIONAL PARK

DUNKERY HILL

4km

GRID REF SS 836 464 (**OS**181)

LENGTH 4970m

HEIGHT GAIN 372m

APPROX CLIMB TIME 22mins

5 DUNKERY BEACON

This corner of Exmoor is hill-climbing heaven, with a plethora of nasty steep roads to grind up and fly down. It's hard to single out one climb that sets itself apart from all others, but the road heading away from Luccombe up to the Beacon is a beast. Leave the crossroads and head into thick forest. Ramping up straight away at 17% and winding across a steep cattle grid, you ride upwards under the trees. The opening stretch over, your legs will already be burning by the time the gradient affords you a brief rest before it climbs again, and if you thought the first part was hard, think again. A perfect stretch of unrelenting 17% gradient cuts its way through the gorse, turning left, steeper, right, steeper still and delivering you to the finale. Ahead, the road winds like a streamer dropped from a tall building, kinking left and right, left, right, steep all the way. You'll finish, consumed by fatigue, adjacent to a small stone carpark.

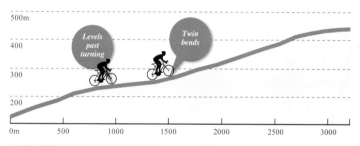

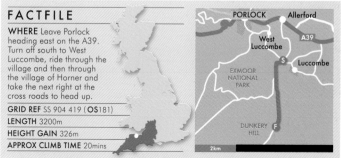

FACTFILE

WHERE Leave Porlock heading east on the A39. Turn off south to West Luccombe, ride through the village and then through the village of Horner and take the next right at the cross roads to head up.

GRID REF SS 904 419 (**OS**181)

LENGTH 3200m

HEIGHT GAIN 326m

APPROX CLIMB TIME 20mins

6 EXMOOR FOREST

LYNMOUTH, DEVON

The town of Lynmouth lies at the base of three stiff climbs – the very tough Countisbury Hill, the shorter and steeper Lynton Hill and finally the long road heading up onto Exmoor. It's this route from sea level to the top of Hoar Tor that provides the most climbing. A tiny kick out of town soon eases into a steady gradient as the road follows the river through the valley. Past a car park, you reach the left turn for the B3223 and cross the bridge onto the harder inclines. You wouldn't expect to reach the top of Exmoor without some serious toil and this middle stretch gives you that. Keep pushing and you'll reach a couple of hairpin bends, first left, then back on yourself, then right, they deliver you onto the gentler higher slopes. Now above the trees, the well surfaced but rough-topped road, populated by ruminating sheep, grinds on and on, finally topping out just before Blackpitts Gate.

FACTFILE

WHERE Leave Lynmouth on the A39 Watersmeet Road through the gorge. Turn left at Hillsford Bridge onto the B3223 Scobhill Road and continue to head south onto the moor.

GRID REF SS 764 422 (**OS**180)

LENGTH 10900m

HEIGHT GAIN 406m

APPROX CLIMB TIME 25mins

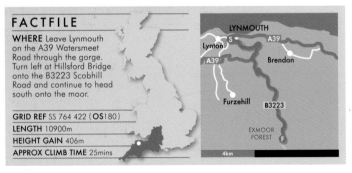

7 CHALLACOMBE

WOOLACOMBE, DEVON

Like so many coastal villages, Woolacombe lies hemmed in next to the sea by the surrounding cliffs, the only access to them being the steep roads that pick their way to the shore. Challacombe Hill is one of the steepest, and it's been used for races for many years. During the summer you'll find it busy with people pushing their hire bikes up to the campsites at the top, having enjoyed an exhilarating ride to the beach that morning. Start the climb just out of town, pass several caravan parks and bend right. The road climbs steep and hard immediately and never lets up. The singletrack, well-surfaced road creeps away from the bustle of the small town, kinking left slightly around midway. Higher up it hits 25% in places and the tarmac begins to ripple, resembling wavelets on the shore below. You'll find it very hard going as you are jolted along the final metres that rise to the top.

FACTFILE

WHERE Leave the Esplanade in Woolacombe and head south on Challacombe Hill Road.

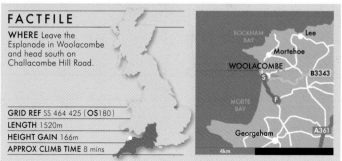

GRID REF SS 464 425 (OS180)

LENGTH 1520m

HEIGHT GAIN 166m

APPROX CLIMB TIME 8 mins

Tucked away in the south-east corner of Dartmoor, amidst a labyrinth of valleys lies the tiny village of Dartmeet, home to Badger's Holt, the place where the east and west tributaries of the River Dart meet. This part of the country is hill-climbing paradise. Cyclists could spend days here and not ride the same hill twice. What doesn't go up steep comes down steep, there's not an inch of flat and to top it all it's set in stunningly beautiful scenery. Spoilt for choice, it's hard to favour one climb over another but the road away from Badger's Holt and up over Yar Tor is a real killer: 20% from the gun, it takes off up the hillside, twisting slightly left then right with very little deviation in direction or gradient. Well-surfaced and well-marked, there's a couple of kinks before you reach the brow and finish adjacent to a car park surrounded by sheep, cattle and the famous wild Dartmoor ponies.

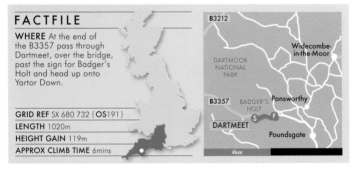

FACTFILE

WHERE At the end of the B3357 pass through Dartmeet, over the bridge, past the sign for Badger's Holt and head up onto Yartor Down.

GRID REF SX 680 732 (OS191)
LENGTH 1020m
HEIGHT GAIN 119m
APPROX CLIMB TIME 6mins

9 HAYTOR VALE

BOVEY TRACEY, DEVON

Rising up the easten side of Dartmoor is the long climb to Haytor Rocks. Beginning just outside Bovey Tracey, the B3387 forks left at Five Wyches Cross. Rising up to 12%, the rough lower slopes are by and large tree-covered but passing the Edgemoor Hotel you emerge out from under the protection of the trees and the gradient steadies, but not enough for you to relax. Ullacombe Farm signals the end of the easier stuff and the road bends left, across a cattle grid and rises steeply into the National Park. Really hard going through a small wooded section, then easing once more before hitting the hardest stretch. A long tough grind brings you out onto open moor from where you climb gently towards and past the Haytor Center, the base for walkers and climbers visiting the giant granite outcrop that towers above your final strength-sapping push to the rugged summit.

FACTFILE

WHERE Head west away from Bovey Tracey on the B3387 Marlborough Terrace and bare left at Five Wyches Cross, continuing on the B3387 to the summit.

GRID REF SX 758 767 (**OS**191)	
LENGTH 5400m	
HEIGHT GAIN 335m	
APPROX CLIMB TIME 22mins	

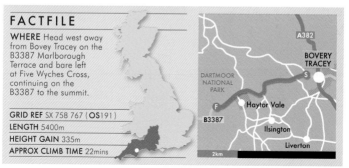

RATING

7/10

10 WIDECOMBE

WIDECOMBE-IN-THE-MOOR, DEVON

Being the region's tourist hub, it seems every second building in Widecombe is selling souvenirs of one sort or another. If souvenirs aren't what you are looking for, but screaming legs and burning lungs are, then you're in the right place for them too. The climb out of Widecombe is the jewel in Dartmoor's crown, a well marked and well surfaced road that hides none of its challenge from you. Leave the village, cross the East Webburn River and get stuck into the steep incline. With no corners, just a brief dogleg deviation, the constant, remorseless 1-in-6 gradient doesn't give you a second's respite. The summit is in view almost the whole of the way up to the car park on the exposed Bonehill Down. The scene for the 1990 National Hill-Climb Championships, it took the great Chris Boardman just 4 minutes 10 seconds to conquer this beast. If you can scale it in twice that then you'll be going well.

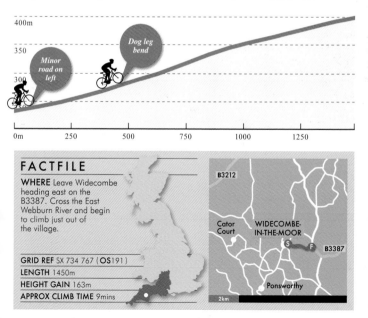

FACTFILE

WHERE Leave Widecombe heading east on the B3387. Cross the East Webburn River and begin to climb just out of the village.

GRID REF SX 734 767 (**OS**191)	
LENGTH 1450m	
HEIGHT GAIN 163m	
APPROX CLIMB TIME 9mins	

11 RUNDLESTONE

TAVISTOCK, DEVON

This climb takes you in stages of varying gradient to the very top of Dartmoor. Begining with a sharp kick out of Tavistock, the B3357 then eases for a while. Still climbing but only gently, you bump along the rough surface under trees and approach the first portion of pain. Take your momentum onto the silky-smooth 15% gradient, climbing hard then banking right across a cattle grid. Next, veer left and as you reach a brow you will see TV mast far in the distance – this is your goal. Enjoy the middle section of all but flat road, then drop sharply at Merrivale, bend right, cross the river, then immediately left and up again. Your legs will burn as the effort kicks in once more, through a couple of 12% corners and you are over the steepest climbing with just the gentle but still not easy upper slopes to the base of the private road that leads to the tower.

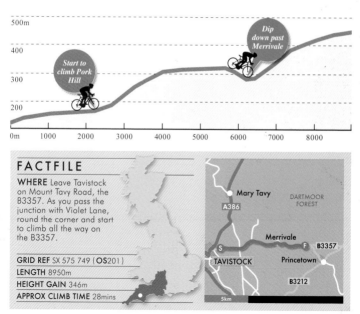

FACTFILE

WHERE Leave Tavistock on Mount Tavy Road, the B3357. As you pass the junction with Violet Lane, round the corner and start to climb all the way on the B3357.

GRID REF SX 575 749 (**OS**201)	
LENGTH 8950m	
HEIGHT GAIN 346m	
APPROX CLIMB TIME 28mins	

12 SALCOMBE HILL

SIDMOUTH, DEVON

All roads out of Sidmouth head upwards but the two either side of the town are of particular note. Heading west is Peak Hill, used for the 2007 National Hill-Climb Championship, while heading east is Salcombe Hill. Peak Hill rises from the bustling seafront, bypassing busy car parks that get extremely crowded in summer, so head for Salcombe Hill. An equally steep ascent, it is perhaps a little shorter, but much quieter. Start your ascent on Salcombe Road and climb past the houses lining the steep early slopes heading towards the observatory at the summit. The road soon bends left into thick tree cover. As you climb, so the canopy rises, and soon you're enveloped by giant old trees either side, their branches arching and meeting high above, creating a cathedral-like space. These murky, quiet and chilly upper slopes reach 20% in places but soon slacken off as the road bends right to level out at a car park.

FACTFILE

WHERE From the centre of Sidmouth, leave the A375, Vicarage Road, and turn east onto Salcombe Road. Over the river take your first left onto Sid Row, then your next right onto Salcombe Hill Road and climb.

GRID REF SY 139 881 (**OS**192)

LENGTH 1210m

HEIGHT GAIN 159m

APPROX CLIMB TIME 8.5mins

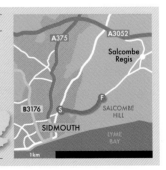

13 DOVER'S HILL

CHIPPING CAMPDEN, GLOUCESTERSHIRE

RATING 5/10

Deep in the beautiful Cotswolds, this little road has been used for numerous National Hill Climb Championships. Although not the steepest of climbs, its popularity probably lies in its central location and pleasant surroundings. One of a number of decent hills in the area, start your climb from Weston-sub-Edge and head south up the ridge, passing the church and the picture postcard stone houses lining the road rising out of the village. Dotted with drainage grilles, the road kinks left then climbs harder up to a sharp right into a tunnel created by the overhanging canopy of branches. The roads surface begins to break up here, but the climb never becomes too extreme, with a maximum 14% gradient. The surface continues to deteriorate as it gradually arcs left, leaving the trees behind as it nears the summit. The road's topping, now lumpy, re-enters tree cover as the gradient ebbs towards the crest at the Dover's Hill car park.

FACTFILE

WHERE Head south out of Weston-sub-Edge and up the ridge.

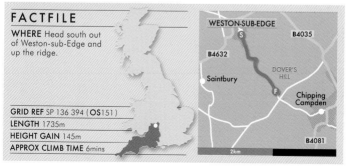

GRID REF SP 136 394 (OS151)

LENGTH 1735m

HEIGHT GAIN 145m

APPROX CLIMB TIME 6mins

SOUTH-EAST

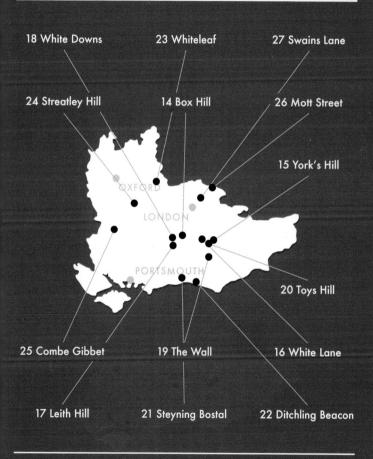

18 White Downs

23 Whiteleaf

27 Swains Lane

24 Streatley Hill

14 Box Hill

26 Mott Street

15 York's Hill

OXFORD

LONDON

20 Toys Hill

PORTSMOUTH

25 Combe Gibbet

19 The Wall

16 White Lane

17 Leith Hill

21 Steyning Bostal

22 Ditchling Beacon

RATING
3/10

14 BOX HILL

DORKING, SURREY

The Alpe d'Huez of the south-east is a favourite climb for many cyclists, and one much-loved for its beautiful setting and challenging but never too testing gradient. Rain or shine, day or night, you are guaranteed company as cyclists of all abilities use its slopes to test their legs. The wonderfully named Zig Zag Road leaves the short B2209 that climbs from Rykers Cafe, and begins its ascent beneath a thick canopy of trees. The gradient is steady but significant then levels briefly at the first hairpin, which has the effect of sling-shotting you around the bend. To maintain speed, hug the left-hand gutter where the surface is smoothest and hold this line to the second hairpin. The road is very rough for the next 200 metres and exits the tree cover to begin the longest stretch. Looking left here you see the valley below before you enter the trees again for the final right-hand bend and push for the cafe at the top.

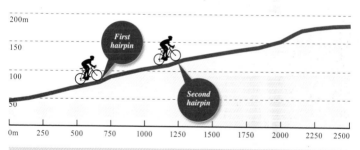

FACTFILE

WHERE Travelling north from Dorking on the A24. At the second roundabout, past Westhumble, exit for Rykers Cafe. Continue up the B2209 then take the first right to begin.

GRID REF TQ 178 513 (OS187)	
LENGTH 2480m	
HEIGHT GAIN 120m	
APPROX CLIMB TIME 7mins	

15 YORK'S HILL

SEVENOAKS, KENT

York's Hill is a climb made famous for being the course of the oldest bike race in the world: the annual Catford Hill-Climb. Each year in October, the final metres of this hill are lined three deep with screaming supporters, willing competitors on as they wrench their bikes up the 20% gradient to the finish line. This testing, twisting climb is even more of a challenge since it has been resurfaced. If there was a scale of road surfaces with pavé (the famous cobbled roads of Northern Europe) scoring 10, York's Hill's new, already deteriorating topping deserves an eight. On top of this, the lower slopes are awash with debris that washes onto the road from the five-metre high tree-lined banks either side, forcing you to search for the cleanest line to get enough traction as the gradient increases. The road switches left to right, left and right again, and relief only comes at the end as you reach Goathurst Common.

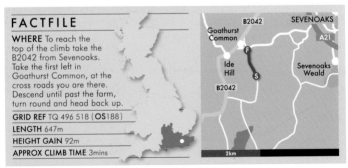

FACTFILE

WHERE To reach the top of the climb take the B2042 from Sevenoaks. Take the first left in Goathurst Common, at the cross roads you are there. Descend until past the farm, turn round and head back up.

GRID REF TQ 496 518 (**OS**188)

LENGTH 647m

HEIGHT GAIN 92m

APPROX CLIMB TIME 3mins

16 WHITE LANE

LIMPSFIELD, SURREY

Known also as 'Titsey Hill' owing to the fact it runs parallel to the B269 of that name, the narrow White Lane is the cyclist's preferred route up this ridge. The climb starts as soon as you leave the main road, rising steeply at first before shallowing slightly, then rearing up with a vengeance near the end. It's a short climb, but a feared one nonetheless, and forms the second half of the annual Catford and Bec CC Hill-Climb races in October. Its surface is rough, pitted and stained white at the edges by the chalk that washes from the surrounding North Downs. Riders are faced with a real struggle to build early momentum as the first two-thirds of the climb are very rough and hard going on the tyres. Following a speed bump-like imperfection caused by poor road maintenance, the surface improves, but here its gradient also increases as it climbs through a tunnel of tree cover to the crest.

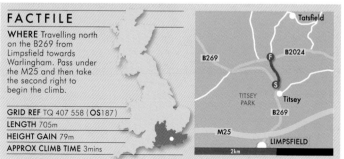

FACTFILE

WHERE Travelling north on the B269 from Limpsfield towards Warlingham. Pass under the M25 and then take the second right to begin the climb.

GRID REF TQ 407 558 (**OS**187)	
LENGTH 705m	
HEIGHT GAIN 79m	
APPROX CLIMB TIME 3mins	

17 LEITH HILL

The proud owner of the highest point in the south-east, at 294 metres above sea level, Leith Hill is one of the longer climbs on the North Downs. It's a road that is raced many times each year, making and breaking riders' reputations in the process. Leaving the B2126 you have a couple of hundred metres in which to choose your gear and prepare for the ascent. Following a footpath on the right, you climb steeply at first and then you are allowed a slight respite before the road's abrasive surface starts eating into your reserves once again. It's steep here and framed with high brick walls that follow the still steepening turns, first right, then left, where you climb towards an intersection of three roads that form a triangle. Bearing left here you have a chance to ease up slightly. But it's not for long, as once again the road climbs and you follow it round to the right, drained from the seemingly endless grind, to the car park on your right.

FACTFILE

WHERE Leaving the A29 at Ockley head west towards Forest Green on the B2126. Take the first right on the apex of a sharp left-hand bend and you are at the base.

GRID REF TQ 130 433 (OS187)

LENGTH 2120m

HEIGHT GAIN 145m

APPROX CLIMB TIME 6.5mins

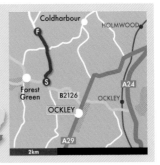

18 WHITE DOWNS

DORKING, SURREY

Starting from the A25 and rising to cross the Pilgrim's Way along the North Downs, White Downs is an obligatory inclusion on local Cyclosportive routes. The road ascends immediately, but what you are presented with at first are best described as two false starts as the road rises, levels out, rises again and then descends. Your heart rate will be up and legs primed, but the climb proper doesn't begin until you cross the railway bridge at roughly halfway. Now it really gets tough as the gradient increases slightly, then – bang! – you're faced with two hairpins, first left, then right, and both 20% at the apex to stop you in your tracks. Next comes a long, gruelling slog up the steep but smooth climb, where the sides of the road are littered with rocks of chalk. As you approach what appears to be the summit you round a final left turn to face another excruciating 50 metres before you have conquered this beast of the south-east.

FACTFILE

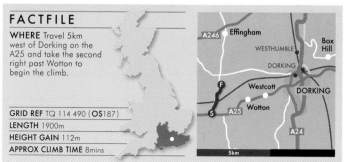

WHERE Travel 5km west of Dorking on the A25 and take the second right past Wotton to begin the climb.

GRID REF TQ 114 490 (OS187)

LENGTH 1900m

HEIGHT GAIN 112m

APPROX CLIMB TIME 8mins

RATING
5/10

19 THE WALL

FOREST ROW, EAST SUSSEX

Kidds Hill, east of Colemans Hatch in East Sussex, has been dubbed The Wall because when you reach the last section that is exactly what it feels like you're faced with. Begin this climb out of Newbridge. Crossing a bridge after a ford the road rises steadily. Bending slightly left it soon straightens and there you have it: The Wall. Dead straight, uniformly steep, the road rises through the trees, no bends, no dips, no mercy. Why deviate when the quickest route to the top is a straight line, in this case one leading to the light at the end of the tunnel of tree cover. Pedal rev by pedal rev you'll drag yourself towards this light, ever brighter as the pain increases, knowing once you reach it your torment will be almost at an end. Into the open, the gradient eases as you enter the beautiful heath on top of the Ashdown Forest with around 100 metres left to finish, just shy of the T-junction with the B2026.

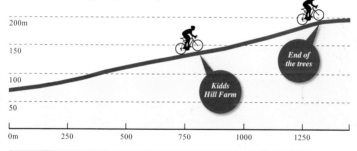

FACTFILE

WHERE Leaving Forest Row just south of East Grinstead head east on the B2110. As you enter Colemans Hatch take the first right and continue straight through to Newbridge to begin the climb.

GRID REF TQ 464 316 (**OS**188)

LENGTH 1440m

HEIGHT GAIN 125m

APPROX CLIMB TIME 4.5mins

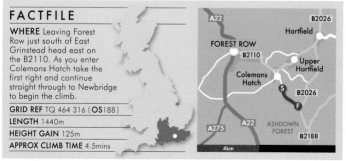

20 TOYS HILL

EDENBRIDGE, KENT

A long, arduous ascent by south-east standards, don't be fooled by its playful name as this climb is as serious as it gets along the North Downs ridge. Leaving the B2042 in the valley, north-east of Edenbridge, Toys Hill bears slightly left, climbing gently at first, with the gradient gradually increasing in definite segments until you hit the final 18% push to the summit. Keep some strength in reserve until you see the village of Toys Hill, where the effort really kicks in. The sting in the tail comes in the shape of 300 metres of dead straight, silky smooth tarmac that saps every last ounce of strength from the legs. As you pass the sloping driveways of the houses on your right, you'll be begging for the end, but it doesn't come easy: there's still a good 200 metres following the steepest section before you can finally relax at the crest adjacent to the Toys Hill car park.

FACTFILE

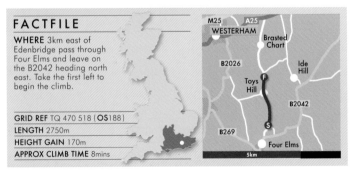

WHERE 3km east of Edenbridge pass through Four Elms and leave on the B2042 heading north east. Take the first left to begin the climb.

GRID REF TQ 470 518 (**OS**188)	
LENGTH 2750m	
HEIGHT GAIN 170m	
APPROX CLIMB TIME 8mins	

SOUTH-EAST

21 STEYNING BOSTAL

STEYNING, WEST SUSSEX

Running up and over the South Downs, Steyning Bostal is the final hurdle for many a ride heading to the coast. There are two ways to begin this climb, both starting from the centre of Steyning and both tough. The route raced each year in the Brighton Mitre CC Hill-Climb uses Bostal Road, the southernmost of the two ascents and the one which usefully avoids a junction. Climbing reasonably steeply to begin with, you soon reach a 17% sign. After crossing several raised ridges the road twists left, then right and is hard going through the bends. It next climbs through woodland then plateaus for a while, giving you just enough time for a brief recovery before you hit the second section – hard left, the road, much smoother here, passes the junction for the alternate beginning before easing slightly. Passing an exposed chalk face on the right, it sweeps left, the gradient easing all the time before it turns right to finish opposite a small car park.

FACTFILE

WHERE Heading south into Steyning on the A283 take the first right turn into the village. Ride almost completely through the village to turn right up Bostal Road then head upwards.

GRID REF TQ 165 099 (OS198)

LENGTH 1620m

HEIGHT GAIN 123m

APPROX CLIMB TIME 6mins

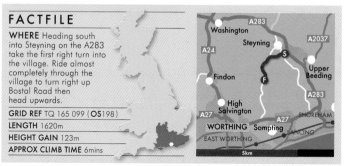

22 DITCHLING BEACON

DITCHLING, EAST SUSSEX

The hill all non cyclists dread, Ditchling, just above Brighton, holds the title of the climb that's forced more riders off their bikes than any other as it's the sting in the tale of the annual London to Brighton charity ride. It has also been included in many races, including the 1994 Tour de France. Heading out of Ditchling, the rough road rises just enough to prime your legs for the climb ahead. Across a junction the road banks left and ramps up steeply as you enter tree cover into the snaking bends. Stepping up, steeper with each turn, choose your line carefully here as the gutter is often littered with debris. Exiting the tree cover the sky opens and the weald stretches in front of you, but this is the mother of all false summits and the pleasant view disappears as suddenly as it appeared and the road bends right into more tree cover, switching again before you emerge into the open, this time to play out the summit scenario for real.

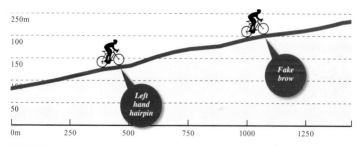

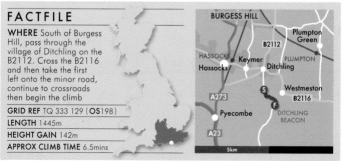

FACTFILE

WHERE South of Burgess Hill, pass through the village of Ditchling on the B2112. Cross the B2116 and then take the first left onto the minor road, continue to crossroads then begin the climb

GRID REF TQ 333 129 (OS198)

LENGTH 1445m

HEIGHT GAIN 142m

APPROX CLIMB TIME 6.5mins

23 WHITELEAF

PRINCES RISBOROUGH, BUCKINGHAMSHIRE

As the cornerstone of one of the country's most famous bike race routes, the Archer Grand Prix, this hill is a must. The inclusion of such a tough hill can really make a race and a race will gain a reputation because of it, attracting strong riders wanting to add their name to the list of winners. You start the ascent by turning off the A4010 from Monks Risborough, climbing from the off. Smooth and straight, the gradient increases gradually up to a left-hand kink where it slackens. The road twists a little, past houses as it makes its way towards where the serious business begins. Banking right, the climb soon hits its 1-in-7 rating and the surface, composed of several toppings in various states of disrepair, gets rougher as the road passes through tree cover. It continues steeply until the final left-hand bend alongside a small shelf of chalk, where you face one final kick before the gradient subsides and you reach the peak adjacent to a right turn.

FACTFILE

WHERE Travelling north east from Princess Risborough on the A4010 reach Monks Risborough. Then take the first right before a school heading towards Whiteleaf.

GRID REF SP 814 043 (**OS**165)	
LENGTH 1420m	
HEIGHT GAIN 127m	
APPROX CLIMB TIME 6mins	

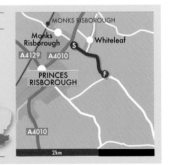

24 STREATLEY HILL

STREATLEY, WEST BERKSHIRE

Streatley Hill is an infamous climb in this region, and a recent inclusion in the professional Tour of Britain only strengthened its status as a classic. Rising from the idyllic villages of Streatley and Goring, as soon as you leave the A417 that bisects them, this unforgiving stretch of road begins to climb. It is steep to the first bend, a slight left, then steeper still for a short section that takes you to the next slight left-hander, where the gradient increases slightly once more. Apart from numerous sunken iron drainage grilles close to the gutter, the surface is good, almost smooth in places. Passing a driveway on the left you reach the final push and the hardest sector. As the road bends right you can picture the summit but have to work very hard to reach it as the road banks left, topping out just past a National Trust car park. Take care here as this is a busy spot with cars turning to enter and exit the car park.

FACTFILE

WHERE Follow the Thames heading north west from Reading along the A329. As the road reaches Streatley take the first and only left turn onto the narrow B4009 and start to climb.

GRID REF SU 591 807 (OS174)

LENGTH 980m

HEIGHT GAIN 130m

APPROX CLIMB TIME 5.5mins

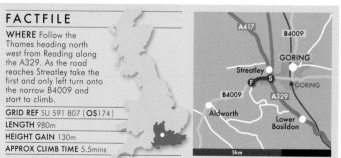

RATING
5/10

25 COMBE GIBBET

HUNGERFORD, WEST BERKSHIRE

With stunning views from the top, Combe Gibbet, or Inkpen Hill, is a real treat to climb. Heading south from the village of Inkpen and into a valley, the climb starts adjacent to an abandoned farm building. Gentle at first, the road continues straight and smooth, but cast your eyes upwards and atop the hill you can see the gibbet. Erected to execute criminals, or more often to display their bodies, it dates from 1676 and adds a sinister context to this beautiful ascent. The gentle rise bends left and climbs fiercely beneath a canopy a trees, where the surface starts to deteriorate. Once out the other side of the tree cover the climb feels easier but it's the surface that has improved, not the gradient that's slackened. The road does ease slightly. But no sooner has it done so than it kicks up again for the hard pull to the top, where you are treated to a fantastic panorama of the Thames Valley, and in an instant forget the effort.

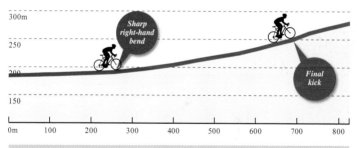

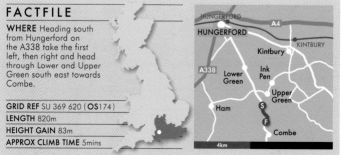

FACTFILE

WHERE Heading south from Hungerford on the A338 take the first left, then right and head through Lower and Upper Green south east towards Combe.

GRID REF SU 369 620 (**OS**174)

LENGTH 820m

HEIGHT GAIN 83m

APPROX CLIMB TIME 5mins

26 MOTT STREET

HIGH BEACH, ESSEX

Just north of London in Essex lies High Beach and the climb of Mott Street. Studying the topography, it's a surprise to find such a tough ascent in this area – there are many shorter hills around but Mott Street is a proper climb. Begin your ascent at a broken bridleway marker just off the A112. The road bends left, passing the junction to Lippets Hill, then rises. A tough opening section flattens where it reaches farm buildings on both sides of the road. A strong whiff of manure is just what you need to propel you up the following lump into the hardest section. The well surfaced stretch of 12% gradient winds past large gated properties on both sides, leveling slightly half way. The final sector heads into tree cover and the brow comes opposite a bridleway, after which there are just a few hundred metres of false flat before the climb ends at the junction of Church Road.

FACTFILE

WHERE To reach the base head north out of Chingford on the A112. When you reach the village of Sewardstone turn right onto Mott Street.

GRID REF TQ 405 977 (**OS**177)

LENGTH 1460m

HEIGHT GAIN 78m

APPROX CLIMB TIME 6.5mins

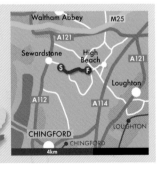

27 SWAINS LANE

HIGHGATE, LONDON

Of the numerous routes up Highgate Hill, Swains Lane is the least travelled by vehicles and one of the city's best kept secrets – for cyclists, that is. Start the climb as the road turns the corner at the base and ride past a right-hand junction. Running alongside Highgate Cemetery the road is smooth and wide, and what little traffic you encounter is likely to be travelling past you as the top of the road is one-way. There is a brief plateau midway past the cemetery gates, then you are plunged into darkness as the gradient kicks up. The road is just wide enough for a single car, with a high wall on the left and thick tree cover overhead. Power up the slope, which touches 20% at its steepest point. Once past a couple of bespoke houses on the left the gradient eases and a large radio mast appears. Pass this and finish at the T-junction with South Grove. You've just conquered Swains Lane – a proper cycling hill in the capital. Priceless!

FACTFILE

WHERE One of the harder hills to find. Ideally use an A-Z, but failing that, head north from Camden to Dartmouth Park and turn right at the roundabout at the base of Highgate West Hill.

GRID REF TQ 283 873 (OS176)

LENGTH 950m

HEIGHT GAIN 71m

APPROX CLIMB TIME 3.5mins

MIDLANDS

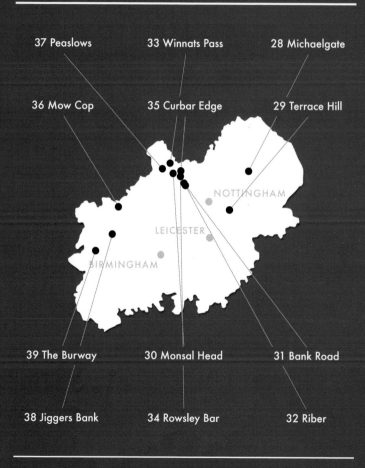

37 Peaslows

33 Winnats Pass

28 Michaelgate

36 Mow Cop

35 Curbar Edge

29 Terrace Hill

NOTTINGHAM

LEICESTER

BIRMINGHAM

39 The Burway

30 Monsal Head

31 Bank Road

38 Jiggers Bank

34 Rowsley Bar

32 Riber

RATING 4/10

28 MICHAELGATE

LINCOLN, LINCOLNSHIRE

Michaelgate is a true classic, a 1-in-6 cobbled road through the heart of Lincoln. The centerpiece of the annual Lincoln Grand Prix, one of the country's greatest bike races, it's a bone shaking, lungbusting test of man and machine. Finding the base of the climb in the maze of little streets can be a challenge in itself as there are a number of cobbled hills including the even steeper but unfortunately pedestrianised Steep Hill. The cobbles are well maintained and even, the key is to keep your momentum and if possible stay seated to increase traction on the often slippery surface. There's a foot of smooth paving between the cobbles and the curb, just enough to ride on, but this takes the fun out of the climb. Once up the main section, you plateau and the way is pedestrianised straight on, so bear left, still on the cobbles to reach the main road, where you turn right to follow the race route into Castle Square.

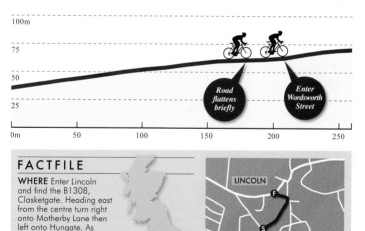

FACTFILE

WHERE Enter Lincoln and find the B1308, Clasketgate. Heading east from the centre turn right onto Motherby Lane then left onto Hungate. As Hungate turns into Spring Hill turn right onto Michaelgate.

GRID REF SK 975 717 (**OS**121)

LENGTH 260m

HEIGHT GAIN 31m

APPROX CLIMB TIME 2mins

29 TERRACE HILL

VALE OF BELVOIR, LEICESTERSHIRE

RATING 1/10

Major hills are rare in this part of the Midlands, so it's not the first destination you'd head to for an epic hilly ride. However, around the borders of Leicestershire, Lincolnshire and Nottinghamshire, the Vale of Belvoir is an oasis of hilly terrain lying in an ocean of flatland. Of all the hills in this area, Terrace Hill best satisfies the criteria for a great climb – a quiet road, a couple of twists and turns, varied terrain and of course an adverse gradient. There's a sense of trepidation as you ride the long approach to the ridge of this ascent with the road disappearing into the trees ahead. Climbing as soon as you enter the wood, the first few metres start steady then head straight up, the good surface leading to a steep right-hand into the hardest section before bearing left. The surface, broken in places, with new toppings ripped up to expose those below, gradually deteriorates before you reach the peak round to the left.

FACTFILE

WHERE Travelling east through Bottesford on the A52 take the first right. Follow the road round and cross the junction to Belvoir. Take the next left to Branston and begin the long approach to Barkestone Wood.

GRID REF SK 798 320 (**OS** 129)

LENGTH 900m

HEIGHT GAIN 76m

APPROX CLIMB TIME 4mins

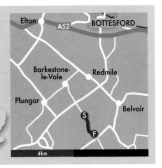

30 MONSAL HEAD

BAKEWELL, DERBYSHIRE

This perfect arc of smooth tarmac takes you from the bank of the River Wye past Monsal Viaduct on your right to the amphitheatre-like finish in front of the Inn at the top. It's not the steepest climb, having a maximum gradient of just 1-in-6, and far from the longest, so Monsal Head is an unremarkable ascent compared to most. But nonetheless it is a favourite hill-climb course, for which the record holder is still the great Malcolm Elliott. Set in 1981, his 1 minute 14.2 seconds has withstood all challenges, so keep this in mind when you set your stopwatch at the bottom. As you start, look carefully and you will spot six inches of repaired road in the left gutter. This super smooth surface will aid your search for speed over the opening section. The gradient is steady the whole way, with no twists and turns, so you have nothing to distract you from your task – force the pedals, round the corner and check your watch: have you beaten the record?

FACTFILE

WHERE North of Bakewell, turn off the A6 at Ashford in the Water onto the A6020. Then take the first left onto the B6465, follow this to Monsal Head. Turn left and descend to the base.

GRID REF SK 184 715 (OS119)

LENGTH 470m

HEIGHT GAIN 57m

APPROX CLIMB TIME 2.5mins

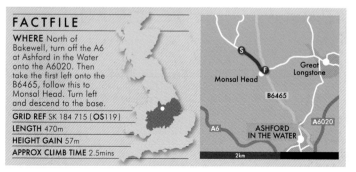

31 BANK ROAD

MATLOCK, DERBYSHIRE

Climbing away from the centre of Matlock, Bank Road is one of the steepest residential roads in England. The venue for the 2008 National Hill Climb Championship turns from a roundabout off the A615 then ramps up abruptly, a straight line of smooth tarmac between the town houses. Beginning around 1-in-6 and getting gradually steeper as it goes, this climb can wear you down like no other. Being an urban road there are numerous drains and parked cars to weave past, as well as markers to focus on, but there's no respite from the relentless slope. Towards the top the road kinks right then left through a steep 1-in-5 section towards a triangular junction. The road opens up here to a large expanse of tarmac; bear right and keep to the far left-hand side where the slope is shallowest, to take as much momentum as possible into the final, gentler section that levels out finally next to a bus stop.

FACTFILE

WHERE Entering Matlock, heading west on the A615 reach the roundabout, travel all around and take the third and steepest exit heading north east.

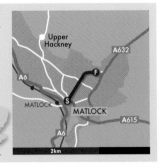

GRID REF SK 305 608 (**OS**119)	
LENGTH 1090m	
HEIGHT GAIN 115m	
APPROX CLIMB TIME 6mins	

MIDLANDS

32 RIBER

MATLOCK, DERBYSHIRE

The road up to Riber Castle out of Matlock is a legendary challenge. It starts climbing from where you turn off the A615, just enough to get the heart thumping and the legs burning over a patchy, lumpy surface. This prelude to the main event flattens for 100 metres and then, off to the right, there it is: Riber Road arcs off the main road like a chute, beginning with an insanely steep 1-in-4 left-hander. There's nothing for it but to build some speed, keep wide to the right, hope there's no traffic and attack the first of five punishing bends. It's brutal all the way, lessening to at best 1-in-6. The second bend sweeps hard right then left to a double hairpin, the third bend arcs left, the fourth – steeper still – takes you into an impossibly tough section, its rough, steep surface doing all it can to bring you to a halt. But the finish is now in sight in the form of the fifth and final bend ahead, 1-in-5 veering left to finish at the crown of the road.

FACTFILE

WHERE Leaving Matlock on the A615 take the second right after the roundabout onto Church Street. Keep climbing then about halfway take the very steep right hand onto Riber Road.

GRID REF SK 305 586 (OS119)

LENGTH 1860m

HEIGHT GAIN 162m

APPROX CLIMB TIME 8.5mins

RATING
8/10

33 WINNATS PASS

For sheer drama, nothing matches Winnats Pass, a winding road through a natural cleft, surrounded by towering, grass-covered limestone pinnacles. Leaving the village of Castleton on the A6187, take a left and begin. The sign says 1-in-5 and so it is, all the way to the top, passing car parks and tourist sites and over what may be the steepest cattle grid in England, where you enter the amazing gorge. The grassy banks either side appear perfectly manicured and form a natural V, with you pedalling right in the centre. The silky smooth surface sweeps gently right before winding slightly and turning left to the summit. With every grinding pedal stroke the banks fade and the sky opens up but the slope never eases, not for a moment. For many years this climb was the cornerstone of the now defunct Tour of the Peak cycle race. To think it was climbed after almost 90 miles of hard racing defies belief.

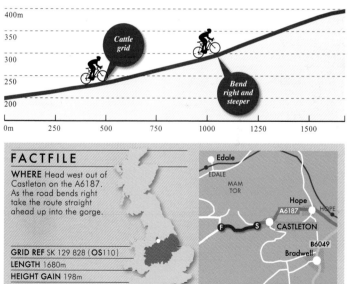

FACTFILE

WHERE Head west out of Castleton on the A6187. As the road bends right take the route straight ahead up into the gorge.

GRID REF SK 129 828 (OS110)
LENGTH 1680m
HEIGHT GAIN 198m
APPROX CLIMB TIME 9mins

34 ROWSLEY BAR

Turn off the A6 into the village of Rowsley and take the first right turn up Chesterfield Lane to begin the climb of Rowsley Bar. Hard from the start, this road's rough surface is dotted with drainage grilles in the gutter and climbs past farm buildings before bending right. Here the gradient eases as you approach a cottage on your left, after which the climb gets much harder. But here there is a rather fortunate feature to note, as at some point roadworks have left a 30-centimetre wide strip of super-silky tarmac running the remaining length of the climb. Unwittingly, this provides the optimum and smoothest route to the summit of this otherwise very abrasive climb. Two hairpins, 1-in-4 at the apex, first left then right, are followed very shortly by another very steep left. Your smooth line eventually veers into the centre of the road as you approach the top, forcing you to leave it and complete the last few metres unaided.

FACTFILE

WHERE Leaving the A6 north of Matlock, turn onto the B6012 into Rowsley. Next take the first right onto Chesterfield Lane and head upwards.

GRID REF SK 279 660 (**OS**119)

LENGTH 1100m

HEIGHT GAIN 140m

APPROX CLIMB TIME 6mins

35 CURBAR EDGE

CURBAR, DERBYSHIRE

Turning off the A623, this climb starts hard, at around 1-in-6, opposite the Bridge Inn. It has a good surface that's smoother on the inside line, which brings you to a steep right before easing. Focus on the phone box up ahead as this marks roughly one-third distance in the centre of Curbar village. Continuing still smoothly and reasonably gently, you pass through the village and head onto the moor via a sweeping left-hander with a dramatic rocky face of gritstone straight before you. Climb on to the steepest part – a tight right-hand bend followed by a winding stretch of 1-in-6 where the surface is lumpier but still good. Once past a couple of car parks on the left, follow the road to a gap in the rocks ahead – a false summit – from where it's not much further to the finish alongside another large car park. A busy spot on weekends, Curbar Edge is a natural multi-purpose sports venue, perfect for climbers, walkers and, of course, cyclists.

FACTFILE

WHERE Heading north from Baslow leave the A623 at the Bridge Inn before you reach Calver. Turn right off the main road, bear left then take the first right to begin the climb.

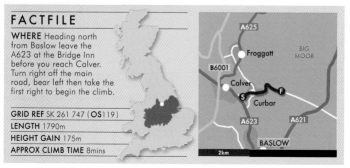

GRID REF SK 261 747 (OS119)

LENGTH 1790m

HEIGHT GAIN 175m

APPROX CLIMB TIME 8mins

36 MOW COP

MOW COP, STAFFORDSHIRE

Mention Mow Cop to cyclists in the West Midlands and their faces may well turn white with fear. The climb's final section is so steep that during sportives photographers position themselves here to capture riders as they topple sideways. To fully test your legs, begin from the railway crossing at its base. Climbing gently past a few houses, the road gets steeper as you bend right then left, then steeper still up to a fake brow. The surface is lumpy and rough but in good condition. Over this brow the gradient lessens, pass a right turn and aim straight ahead at the wall of tarmac you're going to have to scale. Rising dead straight now, increasingly steeper, your destiny awaits in the form of a 25% 200-metre ramp that's just waiting to claim its next victim. Engage your lowest gear, get out of the saddle and force your pedals past the Cheshire View Inn, the proximity of which dramatically emphasises the breathtaking gradient.

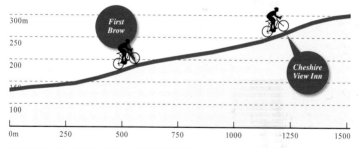

FACTFILE

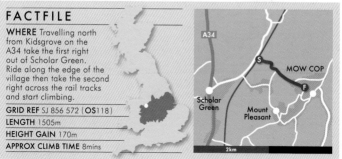

WHERE Travelling north from Kidsgrove on the A34 take the first right out of Scholar Green. Ride along the edge of the village then take the second right across the rail tracks and start climbing.

GRID REF SJ 856 572 (OS118)

LENGTH 1505m

HEIGHT GAIN 170m

APPROX CLIMB TIME 8mins

37 PEASLOWS

CHAPEL-EN-LE-FRITH, DERBYSHIRE

Leaving the tiny village of Blackbrook just off the A6 east of Chapel-en-le-Frith, Peaslows climbs over the ridge to Sparrowpit and into the Peak District National Park. A gradual climb, it's neither too steep nor too shallow. It begins once past a dead end sign over the brook and climbs into a light cover of tall trees. Its well maintained surface has a rough topping but is free of potholes. Once out from under the canopy of trees you soon pass a house on the left, where the scenery opens up. Bordered with stone walls and now dead straight, the rest of the climb is laid before you with no landmarks to aim for but the top, which seems an awfully long way. It's a solid, constant, 1-in-10 drag, with nowhere to recover and no opportunity to alter your pace, making it a slog and grind to the visible summit by what is marked on the map as a reservoir before you can savour the steep descent on the other side.

FACTFILE

WHERE Leaving the center of Chapel-en-le-Frith head east out of town on Sheffield Road. Pass under the A6, take the first right parallel to the A6 then turn left onto Blackbrook Road round the corner and up.

GRID REF SK 085 807 (**OS**119)

LENGTH 1625m

HEIGHT GAIN 172m

APPROX CLIMB TIME 10mins

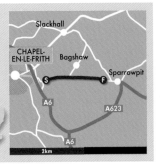

38 JIGGERS BANK

Jiggers Bank rises from the birthplace of the Industrial Revolution, Ironbridge Gorge, a deep scar in the landscape with towering banks either side. Heading north from the bridge you begin the climbing into Coalbrookdale, gently at first away from the valley and the River Severn. Although this is the major route out of the gorge, it's not a busy one, however, there is a set of traffic lights to negotiate at a narrowing in the road so be prepared for a slight delay. Shortly after the lights you have the option to turn left to take a narrow, twisting route up the same ridge, but stick to the larger road for a better climbing experience. Passing under a railway bridge onto Jiggers Bank, the long straight 10% slog out of the gorge leads to a beautifully smooth set of sweeping bends. Passing through these corners, the gradient never slackens. Continue round to the right to the finish, which is even steeper, at the junction with the roundabout.

FACTFILE

WHERE Follow the road through the gorge travelling west from Ironbridge. At a mini roundabout turn right and begin to climb up Dale End towards Coalbrookdale.

GRID REF SJ 664 060 (OS127)

LENGTH 2680m

HEIGHT GAIN 125m

APPROX CLIMB TIME 8mins

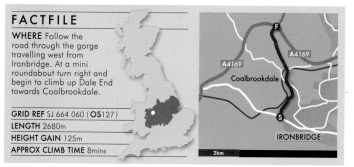

RATING
9/10

39 THE BURWAY

CHURCH STRETTON, SHROPSHIRE

Leave Church Stretton and head east up the minor road onto 'The Longwynd' or 'The Long Mountain' that dominates the skyline. As soon as you start, bending right, you are warned of the 20% gradient ahead. The climb is steep to begin with but levels off slightly past numerous houses, then steeper again as it crosses a cattle grid to enter the wilderness. The coarse but well maintained narrow road rises at 20% like a tarmac ledge perched on the side of the mountain; to the left there's a vertical bank, to the right a precipitous drop. The road veers out of the steepest section with a guard rail offering a little protection from the abyss. From here you enter an easier sector that snakes with the same coarse surface as the earlier slope and leads to a fake brow, from where you may build momentum. The climb isn't over yet though – you still have to pass a couple of car parks to finish alongside the largest one on your right.

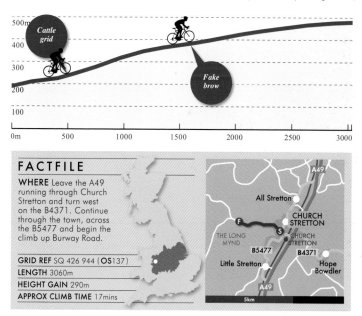

FACTFILE

WHERE Leave the A49 running through Church Stretton and turn west on the B4371. Continue through the town, across the B5477 and begin the climb up Burway Road.

GRID REF SQ 426 944 (**OS**137)

LENGTH 3060m

HEIGHT GAIN 290m

APPROX CLIMB TIME 17mins

YORKSHIRE

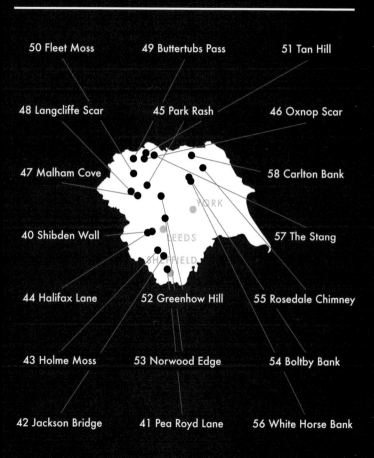

50 Fleet Moss

49 Buttertubs Pass

51 Tan Hill

48 Langcliffe Scar

45 Park Rash

46 Oxnop Scar

47 Malham Cove

58 Carlton Bank

YORK

40 Shibden Wall

LEEDS

57 The Stang

SHEFFIELD

44 Halifax Lane

52 Greenhow Hill

55 Rosedale Chimney

43 Holme Moss

53 Norwood Edge

54 Boltby Bank

42 Jackson Bridge

41 Pea Royd Lane

56 White Horse Bank

RATING

8/10

40 SHIBDEN WALL

HALIFAX, WEST YORKSHIRE

Wow, what a climb – hidden in the valleys north of Halifax lies Lee Lane, or the Shibden Wall. It's a road that has played host to the Milk Race many years ago. Leave the flat valley and begin the climb over a small bridge. The lower slopes are paved and although testing they are just the warm-up for what lies ahead. Passing the 1-in-4 sign the road bends slightly to the left and brings you up to the cobbles, steep at first but manageable. Bend right then approach an incredible left-hand bend that's all but vertical at its apex, forcing you wide to where the cobbles have deteriorated leaving gaps big enough to swallow bike tyres. Alongside the houses the surface improves where the gaps have been filled, but once past the houses and the gaps return. Still very steep, you bounce from stone to stone, island to island, keeping your wheels shy of the crevices between, each jump taking you closer to the summit.

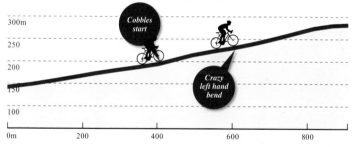

Cobbles start

Crazy left hand bend

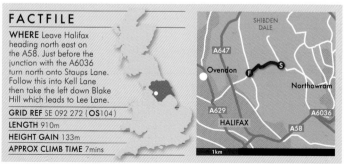

FACTFILE

WHERE Leave Halifax heading north east on the A58. Just before the junction with the A6036 turn north onto Staups Lane. Follow this into Kell Lane then take the left down Blake Hill which leads to Lee Lane.

GRID REF SE 092 272 (**OS**104)

LENGTH 910m

HEIGHT GAIN 133m

APPROX CLIMB TIME 7mins

41 PEA ROYD LANE

STOCKSBRIDGE, SHEFFIELD

RATING 8/10

This unforgiving patchy stretch of tarmac will take you from industrial valley to peaceful moorland in around seven lung-busting, leg-burning minutes. Leaving the B6088 and rising from the heart of Stocksbridge, the venue for the annual Thurcroft CC Hill-Climb is a varied and very tough test. Rough to begin with as you head up past the run-down factories, the road shallows slightly before turning right, onto Pea Royd Lane. Here you hit the first sector of 20%, the surface is terrible and gets worse, but round the next left and everything improves. Crossing the bridge over the A616 the gradient shallows as you join a section of new tarmac but, once over, it rises again with a vengeance. Here you take another 20% left-hander to hit the final stretch, twisting left, then right, over a fake brow, you still have a substantial distance until the road peaks finally, framed in a V by high stone walls either side.

FACTFILE

WHERE Leave the B6088 midway through Stocksbridge heading north on Hunshelf Road. Drop down, cross the roundabout then head left continuing on Hunshelf Road and up the hill.

GRID REF SK 272 993 (**OS**110)

LENGTH 1180m

HEIGHT GAIN 145m

APPROX CLIMB TIME 7mins

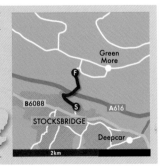

Green More

F

B6088   A616

S

STOCKSBRIDGE

Deepcar

2km

42 JACKSON BRIDGE

Turning off the A616 and rising out of Jackson Bridge just south of Holmfirth is the winding Kirklees Way, commonly known in hill-climbing circles as Jackson Bridge. The former National Hill-Climb course up to Tinker's Monument is varied in its gradient but never easy. Leaving the valley, the even surface climbs past houses on your left and right away you're into the hardest stretch. A triple whammy of 20% bends, right, left then right again will all but bring you to a standstill. Once through this section the slope lessens as you pass cottages and reach a T-junction. Continuing up the coarse surface, the steepness ebbs and flows as the road winds its way. Before the final stretch there is a small dip – a mere 20 metres of relief, but oh so welcome. A moment's relief, and speed gained, but the harshness of the following right-hander robs you of any momentum and you are left to grind it out right up to the farm at the top.

FACTFILE

WHERE Heading north on the A616 pass Hepworth and enter Jackson Bridge. At a cross roads before a sharp left-hand bend turn right onto South View then left onto Tenter Hill Road and up.

GRID REF SE 176 072 (OS110)

LENGTH 1510m

HEIGHT GAIN 161m

APPROX CLIMB TIME 9mins

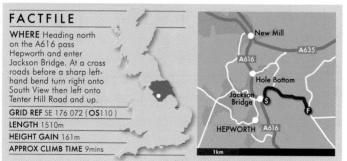

43 HOLME MOSS

HOLMFIRTH, KIRKLEES

Leaving Holmfirth and passing through Hinchcliffe Mill and Holmbridge, the A6024 Woodhead Road reaches Holme and shortly after dips left over a bridge before starting its ascent over Holme Moss. This is a major route over the Pennines, and this is reflected in both the quality of the surface and the plethora of road markings designed to curb the speed of motorists. Much like a computer game being played out in real life, you are bombarded with signals to slow, arrows marking direction and, more usefully, markers counting down the distance to the exposed summit. Starting from the mile mark, these will take you all the way to the 200- and finally 100-meter marks, and are presumably left over from one of the major races that has passed over this climb. Never too steep, at 10%-12% all the way, Holme Moss is nevertheless hard and the top is always in view, leaving you under no illusions about the effort needed to reach it.

FACTFILE

WHERE Head east from the centre of Holmfirth on the A6024. Pass through the villages of Holmbridge and Holme then begin to climb as the road bends left over a bridge.

GRID REF SE 097 036 (**OS**110)	
LENGTH 2235m	
HEIGHT GAIN 204m	
APPROX CLIMB TIME 11mins	

44 HALIFAX LANE

LUDDENDEN, CALDERDALE

Leaving the village of Luddenden, this climb combines the three roads that provide the hardest route to the top. The opening, viciously steep section of Halifax Lane is well surfaced, with the left-hand gutter lined with large, dinner-plate sized smooth cobbles. They lie beneath the more recent surfaces, forming what was once a far more challenging surface akin to the famous cobbled climbs of Belgium. This road eases in places but no sooner has it done so that it bites back with another hard section or a 20% corner. Once you turn into Birch Lane, the surface deteriorates and there are a few ironworks. The large cobbles are now on the right-hand side. You reach two 25% hairpin bends and then turn left again into Raw End Road. The surface here is patchy, the moss-covered stone walls are higher, and the landscape opens up as the gradient eventually eases slightly up to the T-junction.

FACTFILE

WHERE Leave the A646 north of Sowerby Bridge and turn onto Luddenden Lane. Continue north until the road forks and take the right fork onto High Street. Next take the second right onto Halifax Lane and begin.

GRID REF SE 053 257 (OS104)

LENGTH 1630m

HEIGHT GAIN 185m

APPROX CLIMB TIME 9mins

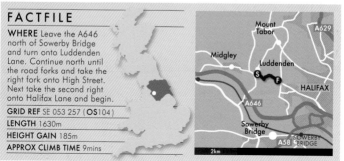

RATING 9/10

45 PARK RASH

KETTLEWELL, YORKSHIRE DALES

Park Rash, a short distance north of Kettlewell, resembles a tarmac ski slope. Following a nasty little climb out of the village you approach the base. Viewed in profile it appears almost 45 degrees but round the bottom bend you realize it isn't quite that steep. Select your lowest gear though and build the momentum necessary to take you through the initial, insanely steep, left- then right-hand bends. You will have no chance to recover as you continue to fight the 18% gradient on what has become a very coarse surface. You are granted a moment's relief once past some farm buildings, where the surface, now smoother, climbs sharply again. There's a reasonable levelling and even a slight dip where you can gather yourself before you head up the final wicked section of 20%. This climb will take you to your limit as you drag your bones over a cattle grid towards the stone marker on your left and finally the summit.

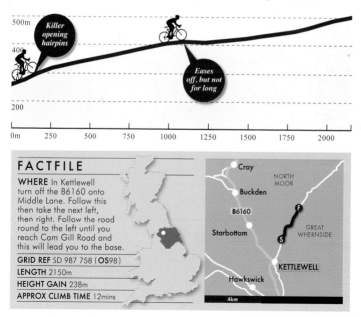

Killer opening hairpins

Eases off, but not for long

500m

400

200

0m   250   500   750   1000   1250   1500   1750   2000

FACTFILE

WHERE In Kettlewell turn off the B6160 onto Middle Lane. Follow this then take the next left, then right. Follow the road round to the left until you reach Cam Gill Road and this will lead you to the base.

GRID REF SD 987 758 (OS98)

LENGTH 2150m

HEIGHT GAIN 238m

APPROX CLIMB TIME 12mins

Cray

NORTH MOOR

Buckden

B6160

Starbottom

GREAT WHERNSIDE

KETTLEWELL

Hawkswick

4km

46 OXNOP SCAR

ASKRIGG, YORKSHIRE DALES

Leaving Swaledale onto Cross Top Road, straight away you hit a 25% right-hand hairpin with a rough and deteriorating surface. This gradient is maintained through a very steep left bend, with the surface on the apex almost unrideable, and here you are forced right, so take care. The climb continues past a farm and bears right. Although the gradient eases here, it is still 18% and it's not until you reach a 350-yard sign that you can back off. From here on the ride is a joy. It has a great surface, climbing, dipping and switching left and right, it's a rollercoaster of a road, always heading upwards but with so many twists and drops that as soon as your momentum is retarded you've a chance to get it back. Push on the short rises, recover on the downs and you will sail to the summit. The surface is somewhat heavy going but is in excellent condition right up to the top past the intersection with a track on your left.

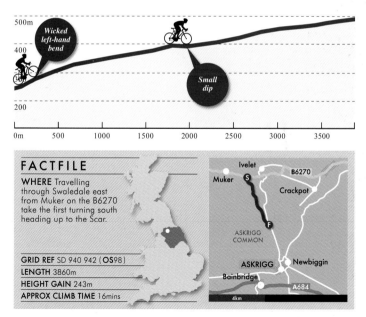

FACTFILE

WHERE Travelling through Swaledale east from Muker on the B6270 take the first turning south heading up to the Scar.

GRID REF SD 940 942 (OS98)

LENGTH 3860m

HEIGHT GAIN 243m

APPROX CLIMB TIME 16mins

47 MALHAM COVE

MALHAM, YORKSHIRE DALES

The harder of the two routes heading north from Malham, Cove Road is a beautiful climb up to Ewe Moor. Leave the village from the triangle of roads opposite the Buck Inn, signposted Arncliffe. Climbing gently from the village, you reach a 1-in-7 sign and the roads rears up, it's snaking narrow path lined with high limestone walls. With Malham Cove, a towering 80-metre high wall of limestone on your right, the road eases then ramps up again, bending right then left then sharp right, a 1-in-5 corner into a stretch of twisting 1-in-6. Right, left, the smooth roads snakes up and up, the only imperfections coming on the tight corners where cars, searching for traction, have damaged the road's surface. Once through the final corners you pass over a cattle grid and can either roll along the flat moor, or turn around to try the alternate route, which, though steeper in places, doesn't offer as tough a challenge.

FACTFILE

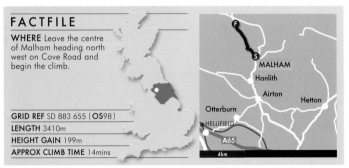

WHERE Leave the centre of Malham heading north west on Cove Road and begin the climb.

GRID REF SD 883 655 (OS98)

LENGTH 3410m

HEIGHT GAIN 199m

APPROX CLIMB TIME 14mins

LANGCLIFFE, YORKSHIRE DALES

Leaving the B6479 just north of Settle, North Yorkshire, this hard climb takes you up and around Langcliffe Scar. The hardest of three similar routes – the others leave Settle to the south and Stainforth to the north – it passes through Langcliffe, where straight away the hard stuff begins up the 1-in-6, up to and over a cattle grid towards a pair of vicious hairpins. After the 1-in-5 gradient through these bends, the road eases back only slightly to 1-in-6, the excellent surface twisting right, then a little further on hard left, again, to 1-in-5 at the apex. With no chance of recovery so far, thankfully a summit is in sight, but it's a false summit. The steep stuff is behind you though, so you can relax somewhat. Now on top of the moor, the road, still with a good surface, rolls very smoothly in places, taking you over a second cattle grid and up to a cut in the rocks before you roll over towards Malham Tarn.

FACTFILE

WHERE Leaving Settle heading north on the B6479 you will reach Langcliffe. Take the first right onto Main Street, follow through the village and as you exit you begin to climb.

GRID REF	SD 839 665 (OS98)
LENGTH	2340m
HEIGHT GAIN	170m
APPROX CLIMB TIME	10mins

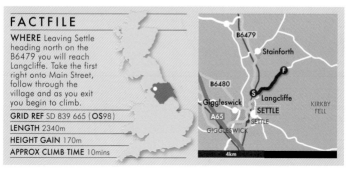

RATING
8/10

49 BUTTERTUBS PASS

The giant Buttertubs Pass is brilliant to climb from either direction. The south side kicks up steep then gradually alleviates as it approaches the top but the north is the toughest, with two sectors of brutal gradient to conquer. Leaving the B6270 from Thwaite, Cliff Gate Road is tough straight away, with a stretch of 14% that, though it eases slightly, doesn't allow for rest. The immaculate surface pulls you towards an Alpine-style zig-zag of hairpins. The gradient is a fearsome 25% here – switching right, left, then right again, you must keep your momentum through these sharp corners, only to be rewarded with a gaping cattle grid, with gaps so large cattle could slip through them. Next, a sharp snaking downhill, the sheer drop to the left fenced off, takes you on to the final section. With the summit in sight you have to heave your bike up yet another 20% section that will have you begging for it to end.

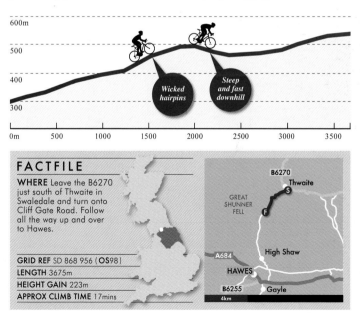

FACTFILE

WHERE Leave the B6270 just south of Thwaite in Swaledale and turn onto Cliff Gate Road. Follow all the way up and over to Hawes.

GRID REF SD 868 956 (**OS**98)	
LENGTH 3675m	
HEIGHT GAIN 223m	
APPROX CLIMB TIME 17mins	

50 FLEET MOSS

HAWES, YORKSHIRE DALES

Fleet Moss, the highest road in Yorkshire, is a beast from either direction but the greater challenge lies in the route south from Hawes. Through Gayle, the road flat, hugging the river, soon rises sharply for a short 17% lung-opener. It then all but levels off as you pass various farm buildings, where the surface is broken and covered with the mud and debris from passing tractor tyres. After a few slight rises the road surface improves dramatically and stretches far into the distance, taking the shortest route over the featureless ridge. Populated by wandering sheep, the road steepens relentlessly, offering nowhere to hide as you click through the gears hoping to find a large enough sprocket just to keep moving. You are eventually rewarded with a blissful flat stretch, but it's not over yet: round a left-hand bend is yet more 20% gradient, a final zig-zag and a few last kicks take you to what feels like the top of the world.

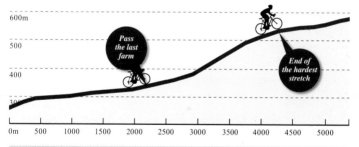

Pass the last farm

End of the hardest stretch

FACTFILE

WHERE Leave the A684 that runs through Hawes and head south on Gayle Lane to Gayle. Pass through the village, over the river, turning right to find the base of Beggarmans Road and head for the sky.

GRID REF SD 862 843 (**OS**98)

LENGTH 5345m

HEIGHT GAIN 323m

APPROX CLIMB TIME 22mins

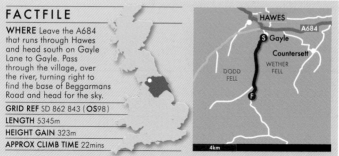

51 TAN HILL

LANGTHWAITE, YORKSHIRE DALES

Leaving Langthwaite and the banks of Arkle Beck, the road up to the Tan Hill Inn is an epic climb by UK standards. The narrow, very well surfaced road, lying like a ribbon draped across a vast expanse of wild grass and gorse, is in many places the only sign of man's presence in this wilderness. Following a lumpy section, the climb really begins after the right-hand turn to the village of Whaw. The gradient is gentle, punctuated with the odd dip or brief bite of 12%, a few bridges and numerous sheep. Windswept and open, this isn't a climb to be challenged in adverse conditions – the featureless Arkengarthdale Moor to your left and Sleightholme Moor to your right would become very hostile in adverse conditions. Climbing on and on and at times flattening out, you come to realise your great height when you see the snow markers lining the road on the final steep section up to the crest and then over to the Tan Hill Inn, the highest pub in Britain.

FACTFILE

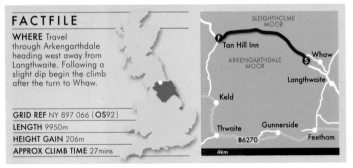

WHERE Travel through Arkengarthdale heading west away from Langthwaite. Following a slight dip begin the climb after the turn to Whaw.

GRID REF NY 897 066 (OS92)	
LENGTH 9950m	
HEIGHT GAIN 206m	
APPROX CLIMB TIME 27mins	

52 GREENHOW HILL

PATELEY BRIDGE, NORTH YORKSHIRE

Here the pain comes in bursts over four distinct stretches of really tough climbing, with brief respite in between. Attack each hard section, get your breath back, spin the legs then attack the next. The climb starts on the flat road through Pateley Bridge. Heading west the road rears up viciously past The Royal Oak pub and out of town. Rising at 18%, this opening stretch is the shortest of the hard sections. The road then plateaus slightly before hitting the second, at 16%. Drag yourself through the woods to reach the third and longest section of hard climbing. Ever so slightly easier, at 15%, the hard stuff alleviates when you pass farm buildings, but still it keeps coming at you. The fourth and final hard section delivers you to the top of the moor. As the gradient relaxes you can see the rest of the climb before you, bending over the brow round to the left with the finish just past the quarry at the sign for Greenhow village.

FACTFILE

WHERE Travelling on the B6265 leave Pateley Bridge heading west. Climb up past the Royal Oak pub and head for the Moor.

GRID REF SE 119 641 (OS99)

LENGTH 3990m

HEIGHT GAIN 282m

APPROX CLIMB TIME 16mins

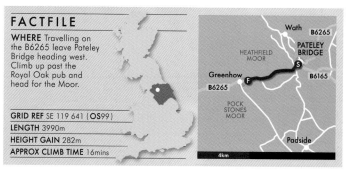

53 NORWOOD EDGE

OTLEY, LEEDS

Crossing the viaduct over the Lindley Wood Reservoir, the B6451 climbs up Norwood Edge in two distinct segments – a sharp abrasive early part followed by a wonderfully smooth, sweeping and long gentle section. The road begins by turning left away from the reservoir. The damaged surface then kinks right and into the hardest section. Dotted with potholes and repair work, this stretch, at 16%, is the toughest of the climb and long enough to make sure you feel the effort in your legs the rest of the way up. Once through the nasty early slopes and out from under the tree cover the road all but flattens as you approach a long left-hander into the Norwood Edge plantation. Once past the car park on your left the road climbs gently, twisting left and right and easing enough to allow a gradual raise in tempo all the way to the finish opposite a Forestry Commission track.

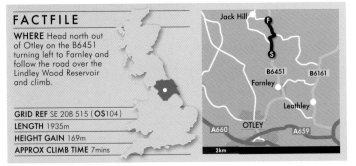

FACTFILE

WHERE Head north out of Otley on the B6451 turning left to Farnley and follow the road over the Lindley Wood Reservoir and climb.

GRID REF SE 208 515 (OS104)

LENGTH 1935m

HEIGHT GAIN 169m

APPROX CLIMB TIME 7mins

54 BOLTBY BANK

BOLTBY, NORTH YORKSHIRE

Approaching the North Yorkshire Moors from the east I am reminded of Arthur Conan Doyle's *The Lost World*. The high plateau rises abruptly from the plains and you just know there's a tough climb ahead. Arguably the hardest route up is Sneck Yate Bank, more commonly known as Boltby Bank. Leaving the village of Boltby, ride over a small hill, round a left-hand bend and you're at the climb's base. The going is easy for a hundred metres, then you're into some steep stuff, the first forays taking you a couple of steps up to the turning for Hesketh Grange. Here the road kinks left and right and then eases to deliver you to the meat of the climb. It's a real tough slog, 1-in-6 and 1-in-5 all the way and the steeper it gets the worse the surface becomes, where struggling vehicles' tyres have torn away the tarmac. At the end of this grind there's a tight right-hand bend, one more kick of 1-in-5 and then you round a final left-hander to level out.

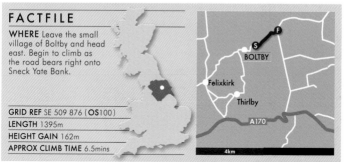

FACTFILE

WHERE Leave the small village of Boltby and head east. Begin to climb as the road bears right onto Sneck Yate Bank.

GRID REF SE 509 876 (**OS**100)

LENGTH 1395m

HEIGHT GAIN 162m

APPROX CLIMB TIME 6.5mins

RATING
10/10

55 ROSEDALE CHIMNEY

ROSEDALE ABBEY, NORTH YORKSHIRE MOORS

Few climbs have such a fearsome reputation as Rosedale Chimney, and rightly so as I snapped my chain not once but twice in my attempt to conquer this vicious stretch of tarmac. Leaving Rosedale Abbey, a sign warns you of the 1-in-3 – yes, 1-in-3 – gradient to come. This climb isn't for the faint-hearted. The surface is rough at first and steep from the outset, but improves as you pass over a cattlegrid and approach the double hairpin. The second bend here is so steep on the inside that it forces you far right, so take care. Now straightening up, the next stretch is ridiculously hard, the main problem here being just staying upright while either side of the road, sheep wait to see if yet another rider falls victim to the Chimney. Stick with it, as eventually the 1-in-3 does turn into a relatively gentle 1-in-6, allowing you to build a little momentum to drag your bike up onto the moor.

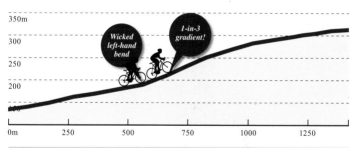

FACTFILE

WHERE From the bottom left corner of Rosedale Abbey leave the main road and turn south east onto Gill Lane, pass the giant warning sign, and head up.

GRID REF SE 720 945 (OS94)

LENGTH 1430m

HEIGHT GAIN 179m

APPROX CLIMB TIME 9mins

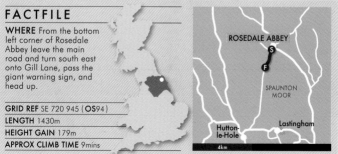

56 WHITE HORSE BANK

KILBURN, NORTH YORKSHIRE MOORS

East of Thirsk lie the Hambleton Hills and the border of the North Yorkshire Moors. Here, if you take the A170 you will encounter Sutton Bank, one of the steepest sections of A-road in the UK. This is a difficult, nasty stretch of road, often clogged with struggling vehicles, making it a horrible trial to ride. The best way to climb this ridge is to take the minor road north from Kilburn and up White Horse Bank. In the shadow of the horse, the ascent starts smooth and steady but soon corners left then right at a severe 20% before easing slightly. The steep surface, deteriorated in places, twists and turns on its approach to a large car park on the left. The gradient then eases briefly before turning right, steeper once more as the now pothole plagued narrowing road brings you to a sharp left, then a final 25% kink left and right before you can relax on the flat smooth surface as you approach to the gliding club up on the left.

FACTFILE

WHERE Head north out of the small village of Kilburn on Carr Lane and simply take your first left onto Low Town Bank Road to head up to the top of the ridge.

GRID REF SE 516 814 (**OS**100)	
LENGTH 1650m	
HEIGHT GAIN 175m	
APPROX CLIMB TIME 9mins	

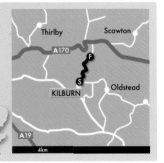

57 THE STANG

LANGTHWAITE, NORTH YORKSHIRE

The road between Arkengarthdale and Barnard Castle takes you up over moorland and through Stang Forest. It's tough from either direction, and although it has 30 metres less climbing I have focussed on the southern side, which lacks the sharp switchbacks of the climb on the northern side through the forest but arguably provides a better climbing experience. From Langthwaite, cross Eskeleth Bridge onto the hard, well surfaced section of 1-in-6 up Stang Lane, which takes you out of the valley below up to a cattle grid. The gradient stays the same up to the car park on the left, by which point the hardest work is behind you. Following a slight downhill you can see the rest of the climb snake up and over the moor in front of you. The surface, smooth where traffic has worn the topping, climbs steadily, dips slightly, then ascends hard up to the exposed top and the border of Yorkshire and County Durham.

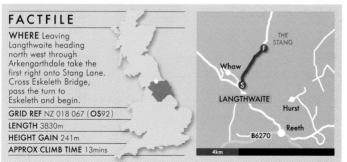

FACTFILE

WHERE Leaving Langthwaite heading north west through Arkengarthdale take the first right onto Stang Lane. Cross Eskeleth Bridge, pass the turn to Eskeleth and begin.

GRID REF NZ 018 067 (**OS**92)

LENGTH 3830m

HEIGHT GAIN 241m

APPROX CLIMB TIME 13mins

58 CARLTON BANK

CARLTON-IN-CLEVELAND, NORTH YORKSHIRE

At the top side of the North Yorkshire Moors, Carlton Bank takes you from the industrial plains of Teeside up onto Cringle Moor. The slight gradient is rough and potholed to begin with, but climbs sharply once past the cattle grid, with the Bank looming above, a black monolith of heather-covered rock. Following a hard left-hand bend the road eases before climbing steeply once again, this time on an improved surface. Next, a sharp right is followed by another gentle right, bringing you to the hardest section. With the Bank over your right shoulder, and a precipitous drop to your left, the surface is now terrible: steep, veering right and deteriorating as it climbs alongside a stone wall that acts as a barrier to the vertical drop. You can now see the summit and will need to pick the best line across the broken surface to the brow, from where you can turn around for an amazing view.

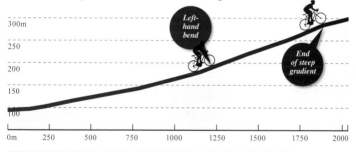

FACTFILE

WHERE Head south from the A172, pass through Carlton-in-Cleveland. As you exit the village turn left onto Alum House Lane and head up.

GRID REF NZ 522 030 (OS93)

LENGTH 2050m

HEIGHT GAIN 202m

APPROX CLIMB TIME 7mins

THE HILL CLIMB

Ten...
That's the moment you know it's real,
the time keeper's call of ten seconds to
go. This is happening, you are here, a
waking moment. You're going to have to
attack this hill and force your body into
a place it doesn't want to go to and one
that it will try everything to get out of.
Five...
And five fingers are held in front of you.
All the training, the sacrifice, the self
discipline, watching the scales, the early
nights, this is why, this is it, focus.
Four...
You grip the bars, you look ahead,
you empty your mind.
Three...
You fill your lungs to pack the muscles
with oxygen, you'll need every last drop.
Two...
Focus, you CAN do this, you're GOING
to do this, focus.
One...
Silence.

Go.
Spin at first, your speed has to be
perfect, overdo it at the start and you'll
die a thousand deaths. You know the
course, you know what to do, you can't
think, it's too late for that, there is only
time for action. You have to find the
sweet spot, to float, fueled on adrenalin.
You must preserve your reserves, but
never hold back. Adrenalin doesn't last.

Suddenly you sense the effort, you're
breathing as hard as your heart is beating
fast, you are at your limit. 30 seconds
in and you've reached maximum, the
primaeval instincts that have kept man
alive since before history are now telling
you to stop, to back off, ease up. You
can't listen though, you can't give in,
you have to push. Your eyes focused as
if staring at a singularity, oblivious to
all except the metre of tarmac in front
of you. Don't think, don't rest, push,
take the pain. You are now deep into
oxygen debt, you simply cannot supply
the demand so the body diverts it to
where it's needed most. Your eyes
blur, you begin to lose sensations in
your extremities but there can be no rest.
Time is standing still, it's hyper real, you
are experiencing life in such rich detail,
this is what your body can do, this is
who you are, what you are, push, push.
The crowds shout your name but you
hear no noise, you see the finish line but
it gets no closer, PUSH. You're barely
able to hold yourself up, your legs are
consumed by lactic acid and your lungs
burn, desperate for air. At last there is the
line, the end to eternity, one final lunge,
one final revolution, done. You fall into
the arms of an official, empty, your chest
on fire and your mouth filled with the
metallic taste of blood. You've been to
the edge, it was two minutes that lasted a
lifetime, the Hill-Climb.

NORTH-EAST

61 Winters Gibbet

60 Peth Bank

NEWCASTLE

62 Chapel Fell

59 Crawleyside

RATING
7/10

59 CRAWLEYSIDE

STANHOPE, DURHAM

The village of Stanhope lies in Weardale, with a stiff climb leaving town from either side. The best option, heading north, is the accent through Crawleyside. Climbing steeply from the off and getting gradually steeper, you reach a sweeping right-hand bend. Once past the Crawleyside sign, grind your way up the punishing 20% slopes through the town. The end of the opening section brings a change in gradient and is marked by a cattle grid as you hit the open moor. The gentler gradient doesn't last long as the road kicks up towards a farmhouse on the left. Pass this house, bend right and you're allowed a short breather as the road dips before the flat approach to the finale. The final effort to reach the top of the moor is an arrow straight 14% section followed by a hard right-hand bend. Now all that stands between you and the point at which you can go no higher is some very gentle climbing to exit Weardale.

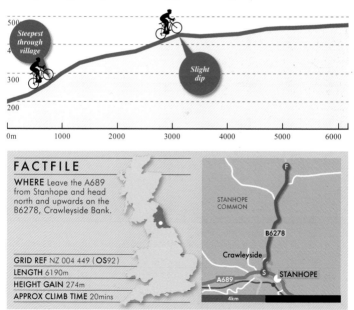

FACTFILE

WHERE Leave the A689 from Stanhope and head north and upwards on the B6278, Crawleyside Bank.

GRID REF NZ 004 449 (**OS**92)
LENGTH 6190m
HEIGHT GAIN 274m
APPROX CLIMB TIME 20mins

60 PETH BANK

LANCHESTER, DURHAM

Leave the centre of Lanchester and head east up the ridge. The climb starts as soon as you leave the main road and the surface is rough with large sunken iron grilles in the gutter. You soon pass a gradient sign and the road ramps up, left, then right. Ride on through the hard, rough 20% bends, then left again to finish this, the hardest stretch at a very damaged fake summit. Continue climbing gently, rising left to another brow, followed by a short dip. Resist the urge to rest here, instead click up a gear to build some momentum for the next section of climbing. An extra few kph when you hit the following testing set of bends pays rich dividends as the gradient bites. As you round the long sweeping right-hander the radio mast at the top will come into view. This marks the summit but it is still some way off; exit this section of bends and there's more gentle climbing to take you there, finishing at the T-junction.

FACTFILE

WHERE Leave the A691 from the centre of Lanchester. Head north east on Peth Bank just south of Station Road past the church.

GRID REF NZ 184 477 (OS88)

LENGTH 1800m

HEIGHT GAIN 141m

APPROX CLIMB TIME 8mins

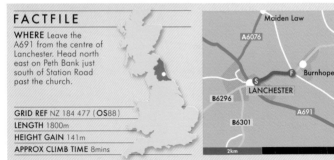

61 WINTERS GIBBET

ELSDON, NORTHUMBERLAND

This climb takes its name from the gibbet at its peak, first erected in 1791 to display body of William Winter. The present gibbet was erected some time later as a curiosity and comes complete with a fake head. Leaving the village of Elsdon, head south-east to start the climb up to the edge of Harwood Forest. Fiendishly, the sharpest stretch is right at the bottom and is sure to make your legs burn with lactic acid, making the rest of the climb that much tougher. The smooth road soon eases, bends left then right. Continue climbing the steady gradient and you will reach a steep left-hand bend up to a fake brow, followed by a short dip. The edge of the road begins to disintegrate here, so ride wide and try to build up some speed to carry you towards the top. Once up the next and final hard stretch and over the brow, you'll eye the gibbet. The hard work is now behind you. Push on up the ever decreasing slope to finish alongside Harwood Forest.

FACTFILE

WHERE Leave the B6341 in the village of Elsdon and head due south over the small Elsdon Bridge. Follow the road round to the left and begin the climb still heading south.

GRID REF NY 962 907 (**OS**80)

LENGTH 3680m

HEIGHT GAIN 153m

APPROX CLIMB TIME 11mins

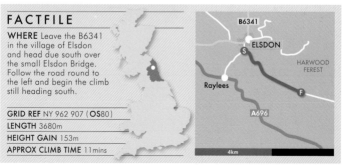

62 CHAPEL FELL

ST JOHN'S CHAPEL, DURHAM

The highest paved pass in England, Chapel Fell comes complete with the tough gradient and frequently wild weather that befits its status. Pick your way out of St John's Chapel, past a row of cottages to meet your first test, short and steep but followed by a drop from where you can see the road that lies ahead. Next, a very sharp dip followed by an identically sharp rise, so no chance to carry any momentum though here as it evaporates as quickly as it was created. Drag yourself from this hollow, easing up to a cattle grid, the start of your killer slog to the summit. Partway along this decent surface is a fake brow where you're allowed a brief moment's rest crossing a bridge. Over the stream is a leg-breaking wrench up, left then right. You'll reach the summit, legs aching and probably battered by the elements. Cross the cattle grid to finish next to the old quarry with nothing between you and the sky.

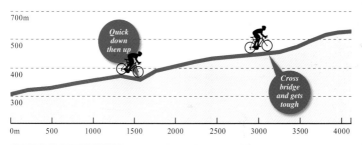

Quick down then up

Cross bridge and gets tough

700m
500
400
300

0m   500   1000   1500   2000   2500   3000   3500   4000

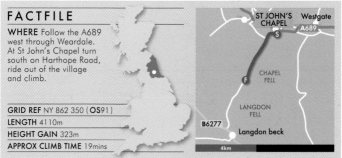

FACTFILE

WHERE Follow the A689 west through Weardale. At St John's Chapel turn south on Harthope Road, ride out of the village and climb.

GRID REF NY 862 350 (**OS**91)

LENGTH 4110m

HEIGHT GAIN 323m

APPROX CLIMB TIME 19mins

ST JOHN'S CHAPEL   Westgate
A689
CHAPEL FELL
LANGDON FELL
B6277
Langdon beck
4km

SCOTLAND

69 Bealach-na-Ba

67 Cairn Gorm

66 The Lecht

INVERNESS

ABERDEEN

64 Cairn
O' Mount

GLASGOW

68 Rest
and be
Thankful

63 Mennock Pass

65 The Cairnwell

63 MENNOCK PASS

Home to Wanlockhead, the highest village in Scotland, the Mennock Pass links the A76 and the M74 over the top of the Lowther Hills. Ridden from the Mennock side, the awesome beauty of this route has to be seen to be believed. Begin the climb from the pan-flat, wide valley floor, whose smooth, steep sides tower above you. The gradient rises through the huddled hills, winding from the base of one to the base of the next. Across a stone bridge the road climbs steeper, cutting its way upwards. There's a small, sinuous downhill around midway, then the road becomes steep again as an antiquated guard rail swaps from the right to the left side of the road. This is a really long climb, never too steep but constantly challenging. By the time you reach Wanlockhead you've all but conquered the Mennock Pass yet there's just a little more to do, taking you past the village before the road heads downhill.

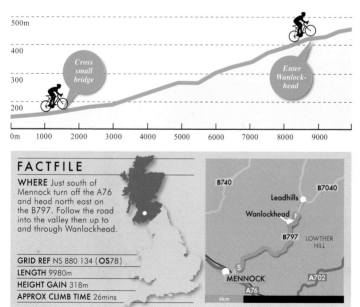

FACTFILE

WHERE Just south of Mennock turn off the A76 and head north east on the B797. Follow the road into the valley then up to and through Wanlockhead.

GRID REF NS 880 134 (**OS78**)

LENGTH 9980m

HEIGHT GAIN 318m

APPROX CLIMB TIME 26mins

64 CAIRN O' MOUNT

A couple of miles north of Fettercain lies the small and welcoming outpost, the Clatterin' Brig tea rooms. Rising sharply from the base of its steep driveway, the B974 heads into the Grampian Mountains to summit at Cairn o' Mount. Beginning hard, at 16%, the reasonably wide road bends left then heads straight up. The gradient eases only slightly as you ascend to a ruined building on your left, its remaining stones just about clinging to the hillside. Bending right past the ruins, the gradient eases for some time and the long middle section runs along a rough but well-surfaced road marked with snow poles. Although far gentler than the start, it is not quite easy enough to allow much recovery as it approaches the 14% top section. Easing right then hard left and again hard right into the final push, you finish alongside a small car park as the road disappears down the other side into Glen Dye.

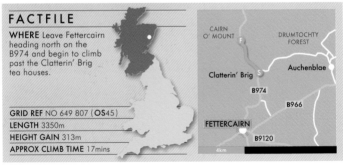

FACTFILE

WHERE Leave Fettercairn heading north on the B974 and begin to climb past the Clatterin' Brig tea houses.

GRID REF NO 649 807 (**OS**45)	
LENGTH 3350m	
HEIGHT GAIN 313m	
APPROX CLIMB TIME 17mins	

CAIRN O' MOUNT
DRUMTOCHTY FOREST
Clatterin' Brig
Auchenblae
B974
B966
FETTERCAIRN
B9120
4km

114

SPITTAL OF GLENSHEE, PERTH AND KINROSS

The Cairnwell is a giant arc of a climb that guides you deep into the Cairngorms National Park. As the principle route north for miles around, the road is often busy but plenty wide enough for cycles and vehicles. Ride past the Spittal of Glenshee, the last settlement for some distance, and head through the beautiful valley approaching the climb. Though you are gaining altitude very gradually, the climbing doesn't truly begin until the road turns right and begins its majestic sweep up into the mountains at 12% from start to finish. You pass 'no stopping' signs on either side of the road, which gently banks left as the stiff gradient pulls you out of the valley. You now enter the long and straight stretch of the climb, the gutter punctuated with deep-set iron grilles. Bending slightly left towards the brow, pass Devil's Elbow on your right and roll over the top, past the Glenshee Ski Centre and into the Cairngorms.

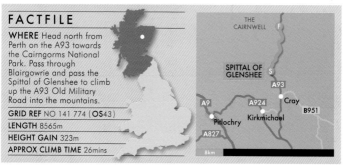

FACTFILE

WHERE Head north from Perth on the A93 towards the Cairngorms National Park. Pass through Blairgowrie and pass the Spittal of Glenshee to climb up the A93 Old Military Road into the mountains.

GRID REF NO 141 774 (OS43)

LENGTH 8565m

HEIGHT GAIN 323m

APPROX CLIMB TIME 26mins

RATING
10/10

66 THE LECHT

A true monster of a climb through the heart of the Cairngorms, the road up to the Lecht Ski Centre is a simply stunning ride. You start your ascent from the beautiful Corgarff castle and straight away you hit 20% slopes – rough, relentlessly steep and twisting a little. Pass through the large orange gates used to close the road in winter – proof, if you hadn't twigged already, that you're heading into serious country. After an age on the opening steep gradient the road banks right to plateau before a brief downhill. What comes next will take your breath away. There, in front of you, painted onto the side of the mountain and looking like a giant flight of stairs, lies the rest of the climb. A short flat section ramps up hard, then almost levels before ramping hard again. Eventually you'll bend around to the left and the battered, rugged road levels for good. In front of you is the Alpine-style Ski Centre, a simply awesome ride.

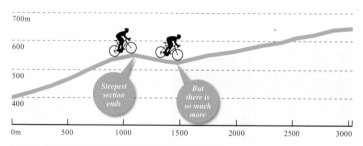

Steepest section ends

But there is so much more

FACTFILE

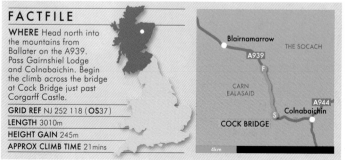

WHERE Head north into the mountains from Ballater on the A939. Pass Gairnshiel Lodge and Colnabaichin. Begin the climb across the bridge at Cock Bridge just past Corgarff Castle.

GRID REF NJ 252 118 (OS37)

LENGTH 3010m

HEIGHT GAIN 245m

APPROX CLIMB TIME 21mins

Blairnamarrow

THE SOCACH

A939

F

CARN EALASAID

Colnabaichin

A944

COCK BRIDGE

4km

67 CAIRN GORM

AVIEMORE, HIGHLAND

A road to nowhere that echos the world's great mountain climbs, this challenge winds up from the valley to finish high at a ski lodge by the base for the mountain railway. More popular with mountain bikers, this climb offers those visiting Aviemore on a road bike a chance to join in the fun. Heading out of town, the long valley road reaches Glenmore, where the real climbing begins. Sweeping left then right, up through the Glenmore Forest, the road climbs hard, winding up and up before banking hard left to level out. Following a sharp right-hander you reach a fork in the road – the begining of a high altitude one-way system. Bear left, climb hard, plateau then follow the road right to climb further then turn left again, where the gradient eases, allowing you to enjoy the amazing views over Aviemore far below. You reach a T-junction; bear left and climb to finish in the large car park for the railway and Ranger's Centre.

FACTFILE

WHERE Head south out of Aviemore on the B9152 and turn south east on the B970. At Coylumbridge turn onto the minor road to the Glenmore Forest Park, past the Glenmore Lodge and then climb.

GRID REF NH 989 062 (OS36)

LENGTH 5400m

HEIGHT GAIN 300m

APPROX CLIMB TIME 22.5mins

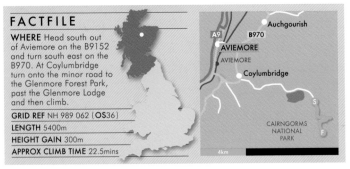

In 1753, a stone was placed at the top of this climb by soldiers who built the first road over the pass, bearing the words 'Rest-and-be-Thankful'. The original stone is long gone and a car park now sits in its place, where the A83 meets the B828. It's a tough climb up the A83 from either direction but the harder, quieter and wilder climb is up the B-road from Hell's Glen. Pedal up the rough, badly damaged singletrack road, you'll find the fluctuating gradient isn't too tough to begin with as frequent level stretches offer the rider respite. As the forest opens up the accent eases, but once you're over a small stone bridge it's solid climbing from here on. Potholed and broken, the road follows the river and throws in a couple of 16% corners, left then very steep right. Leaving the forest and the hardest climbing behind you, roll along to the radio mast at the top, then descend to Rest and be Thankful.

FACTFILE

WHERE Head south out of Cairndow then turn right onto the A815. Just before Ardno turn south onto the B839 into Hell's Glen. Follow this road to the junction, turn hard left and begin to climb.

GRID REF NN 226 067 (OS56)

LENGTH 4450m

HEIGHT GAIN 253m

APPROX CLIMB TIME 17mins

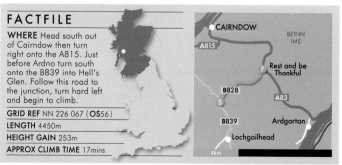

RATING 11/10

69 BEALACH-NA-BA

APPLECROSS, HIGHLAND

This is it: the Holy Grail, the toughest and wildest climb in Britain. Anything you have read or been told about this amazing road is likely to be true. For once, you can believe the hype. The majority of Scotland's roads stick to valleys as there's no need to cross the mountains but here they link the village of Applecross with the rest of the world by taking the route over the top of Bealach-Na-Ba. It is an incredible climb both ways but the road from Tornapress, heading north-west, is just awesome.

Do not attempt to ride here in unfavourable conditions. Check the forecast before you head out and be prepared for harsher weather at the top. Leave the head of Loch Kishorn, turn left and you're on your way, soon passing the large sign warning of the various dangers that lie ahead. It's not too steep to begin with but as the road bends hard left at the base of an almighty tower of rock, then the gradient increases. Now climbing steeply, this slither of rough road clinging precariously to the mountainside bends hard right to deliver you into a true wilderness. Apart from the few cars that travel this route, you're more likely to have wary, onlooking deer for company, as they track your slow progress up the mountain. Up ahead, eventually the final bends come into view, just as the gradient gets brutal on the long weather-beaten 20% slope that tests your legs to the limit. After all that has preceded it, the finale – a set of four hairpin bends – may be all too much, but fear not. The road levels between the sharp bends giving you a chance to attack each wicked corner then gather yourself in time for the next. Zig-zag past cascading waterfalls, amidst the brief protection of rocky outcrops to exit this tangle of tarmac and round one final left hand to finish.

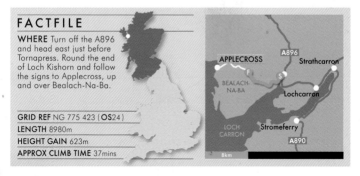

FACTFILE

WHERE Turn off the A896 and head east just before Tornapress. Round the end of Loch Kishorn and follow the signs to Applecross, up and over Bealach-Na-Ba.

GRID REF NG 775 423 (OS24)

LENGTH 8980m

HEIGHT GAIN 623m

APPROX CLIMB TIME 37mins

NORTH-WEST

80 Honister Pass

82 Whinlatter Pass

77 Hartside

81 Newlands Hause

83 Kirkstone Pass

CARLISLE

84 Hardknott Pass

78 Lamps Moss

85 Wrynose Pass

73 Garsdale Head

76 Jubilee Tower

LIVERPOOL

79 Cross of Greet

75 Trough of Bowland

74 Nick of Pendle

71 Swiss Hill

70 Cat and Fiddle

72 The Rake

70 CAT AND FIDDLE

The A537 out of Macclesfield over to Buxton is named after the remote Inn at the top and is a favourite with cyclists and motorcyclists alike. Beginning in the centre of Macclesfield and heading out of town, you gradually leave the congestion and noise behind you. The surface is very rough to begin, sweeping left and right through the wide corners, climbing gently and then flattening briefly at Walker Barn. Road signs designed to slow motorcyclists now adorn most bends, along with countless vivid road markings and other warnings. Steeper now, you enter the Peak District where you have the option to leave the main road and take an alternative route, but stick to the A537. There are numerous twists and turns as you churn up this epic climb. It's never too steep, and even features a couple of sweeping dips on it's way up to Goyt's Moss and the one sign of life in this hostile landscape, the Cat and Fiddle Inn.

FACTFILE

WHERE Begin the climb in the centre of Macclesfield at the junction of the A523 and the A537, Buxton Road. Follow the latter all the way to the Inn at the top.

GRID REF SK 001 718 (**OS**118)

LENGTH 11270m

HEIGHT GAIN 381m

APPROX CLIMB TIME 30mins

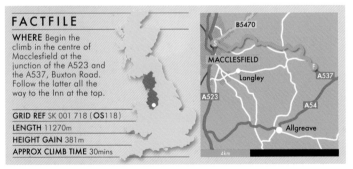

ALDERLEY EDGE, CHESHIRE

Running through the affluent Cheshire town of Alderley Edge is one of only a handful of cobbled roads that still survive in the county and one that will have you fighting more than just the pull of gravity. Rearing up from Mottram Road, the initial section resembles an organised pile of rubble. Traverse this and the pattern of the cobbles become slightly more uniform but never even. Bending slightly left, the centre of the road is overgrown with grass and weeds, forcing the stones apart to create the surface's random profile. Nearing a group of houses, the left-hand side becomes unridable having disintegrated near the gutter, the hill banks right, steeper but slightly smoother now to a T-junction. Take a left into the final short section of cobbles, much larger and neater but no easier to ride on – continue bumping along until you reach the tarmac that takes you to the summit of the climb.

FACTFILE

WHERE From the centre of Alderley Edge follow the A34 travelling south. Turn onto Chapel Road at the junction with the B5087, head due east, then take your second right onto the cobbles.

GRID REF SJ 852 781 (OS118)

LENGTH 516m

HEIGHT GAIN 69m

APPROX CLIMB TIME 4mins

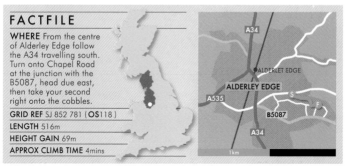

72 THE RAKE

RAMSBOTTOM, LANCASHIRE

A road so steep at the top it has a handrail fixed to the wall to assist pedestrians. Starting on Carr Street, the road climbs incredibly hard straight away and is littered with holes and grilles. Turn sharp left opposite the Rose and Crown pub. The next bumpy and lumpy section narrows and bends round to the right as you weave past parked cars and the gradient eases, but ever so slightly. Dodging yet more holes and ironmongery you approach the final push. Catch your breath if you can to turn right onto Rawsons Rake into the almost impossible 25% stretch to the top. The road, a patchwork of repairs upon repairs, will have you struggling to find a clean line as you grovel up the still narrowing lane into the gloom of tree cover. Finally easing – to 20%! – up past the Holcombe Emmanuel Church, The Rake will have you seeing stars and praying for the torture to end.

FACTFILE

WHERE Leaving Bolton Street, the A676 that bisects Ramsbottom, head west onto Carr Street and start to climb straight away.

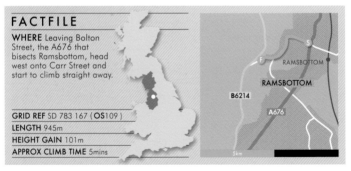

GRID REF SD 783 167 (**OS** 109)

LENGTH 945m

HEIGHT GAIN 101m

APPROX CLIMB TIME 5mins

GARSDALE HEAD, CUMBRIA

Rising from the A648 and climbing gradually to pass under a railway bridge, this is a knarled and hard road on the border of Yorkshire and Cumbria. Past Garsdale Head Station, Coal Road climbs steeper, bending sharp right via a hard 20% corner into the toughest stretch with woodland to the left. The surface is very rough, pitted and lumpy to begin with, but following a slight levelling sections of it have been repaired. Heading on upwards, you are treated here and there to perfectly smooth new tarmac, but the moment your rythmn gets accustomed to the nice surface, along comes another unrepaired stretch, your momentum is dealt a blow and you are reduced once again to bumping and bouncing along. After a long grind comes the false summit, followed by a dip into a smooth descent, then its sharp left before climbing another substantial winding distance to the real summit adjacent to the disused Garsdale coal mines.

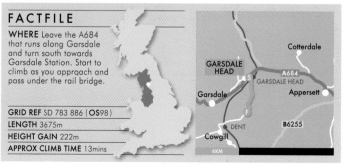

FACTFILE

WHERE Leave the A684 that runs along Garsdale and turn south towards Garsdale Station. Start to climb as you approach and pass under the rail bridge.

GRID REF SD 783 886 (OS98)

LENGTH 3675m

HEIGHT GAIN 222m

APPROX CLIMB TIME 13mins

RATING
6/10

74 NICK OF PENDLE

SABDEN, LANCASHIRE

This famous hill climb venue in the north-west, over Pendleton Moor, has been used to test riders for generations. Leaving Sabden, the Clitheroe Road takes you up the challenging, varied gradient to the 'Nick of Pendle' and the remnants of old quarries. Climbing steeply straight away at 14%, you pass houses on your right and cars to your left with the rough surface, deteriorating at the edges, making it very hard going. Dead straight, cars and houses are soon replaced by grassy verges and gorse bushes and the gradient eases slightly as you approach a large car park.

Passing this you hit the hardest stretch, rising steeper until you reach a cattle grid. With this long hard slog behind you, the road now almost flattens before climbing gently on a brand new surface. Having been punished on the lower slopes, you are now treated to a picturesque zig-zag between steep grassy banks to the summit.

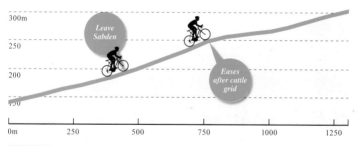

FACTFILE

WHERE Sabden lies midway between Clitheroe and Padiham. Travelling north from Padiham enter Sadben and from its center begin to climb Pendle Hill.

GRID REF SD 771 385 (OS103)

LENGTH 1300m

HEIGHT GAIN 145m

APPROX CLIMB TIME 6.5mins

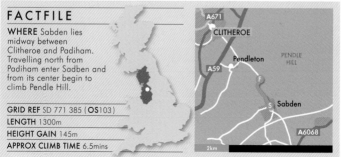

SYKES, FOREST OF BOWLAND, LANCASHIRE

This topographical masterpiece winds its way out of the Forest of Bowland. This Area of Outstanding Natural Beauty (AONB) is a stunning region to ride and its crowning glory is this climb. Heading east along the valley from Sykes Farm and alongside Losterdale Brook, the very smooth road climbs gently as it winds past a weir. Leaving the last farm building the road starts to climb steeper as you enter the 'Trough', a natural basin of multicoloured gorse-covered hills, with this perfectly surfaced road winding up through the centre. Steer clear of the drainage grilles protruding from the gutter and, with no sharp corners to encounter, the only substantial obstacle apart from the significant 1-in-6 gradient is the cattle grid at the summit. Were I asked to create a blueprint for the perfect climb, the Trough of Bowland would be the place I'd start. It just needs to be that bit steeper!

FACTFILE

WHERE If travelling from Clitheroe take the B6478 north then take the turn west at Newton. Travel through Dunsop Bridge and Hareden then you will reach Sykes where the climb begins.

GRID REF SD 622 530 (OS102)

LENGTH 2285m

HEIGHT GAIN 144m

APPROX CLIMB TIME 8mins

FOREST OF BOWLAND

Marshaw

SYKES

SYKES FELL

Hareden

Dunsop Bridge

2km

QUERNMORE, LANCASHIRE

The climb of Jubilee Tower takes you away from the bustle of Lancaster into the beauty of the Bowland Forest. Begin the climb as the minor road, heading south-east, crosses the River Conder and climbs gently as it approaches the village of Quernmore. Levelling slightly before a crossroads, the serious climbing begins after this junction – bending left past a small wood the excellent tarmac next bends steep right into the toughest section. Used in local cycling club hill climbs and often used in the old Tour of Lancashire, follow the sharp right, then left into a long steep 14% stretch up Quernmore Brow. At the end of this grueling drag there's a section of twists and turns up Appletree Farm, where the major climbing is behind you. You've yet to reach the top though, which follows a short downhill, a cattle grid and then a gentle climb to the stone tower constructed in 1897 for Queen Victoria's diamond jubilee.

FACTFILE

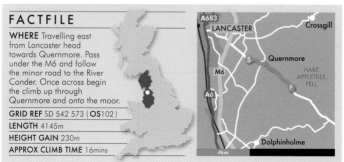

WHERE Travelling east from Lancaster head towards Quernmore. Pass under the M6 and follow the minor road to the River Conder. Once across begin the climb up through Quernmore and onto the moor.

GRID REF SD 542 573 (**OS** 102)

LENGTH 4145m

HEIGHT GAIN 230m

APPROX CLIMB TIME 16mins

77 HARTSIDE

MELMERBY, CUMBRIA

This long climb takes you to the top of the North Pennines and the Hartside Inn. Leave the village of Melmerby, pass the sign warning of possible dangerous conditions, and begin your climb. What this well conditioned road lacks in steep gradient it more than makes up for in distance. Choose your gear, settle into a rhythm and try to maintain it to the top, avoid the urge to change up when the slope lessens but instead let the legs recover for the next inevitable bite in the gradient. To begin with the road constantly twists and turns in and out of woodland. The further you ride, the further the distance between bends, until the scenery opens up – over to your left, a stunning view of the Lake District. Climb on through the empty moor, and soon you'll see the cafe appear on the horizon. A few kinks in the road remain before one final smooth hairpin. Hold your rhythm and push on up to the high-altitude finish.

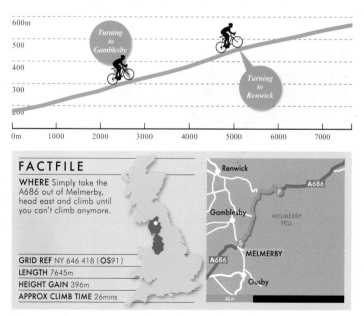

FACTFILE

WHERE Simply take the A686 out of Melmerby, head east and climb until you can't climb anymore.

GRID REF NY 646 418 (**OS**91)
LENGTH 7645m
HEIGHT GAIN 396m
APPROX CLIMB TIME 26mins

78 LAMPS MOSS

Leaving the village of Nateby on the B6270 you are immediately faced with a 20% sign and the prospect of some hard work. Although steep the 20% rating is somewhat of an exaggeration. Following this stiff opening the road bends to the right then levels out, crossing a gaping cattle grid to roll along, affording a respite to the rider. Dip down then climb hard again. Another levelling and you're into a 17% section, twisting slightly and taking you hard past a disused quarry on the left. Now on a very well worn, smooth road you find a long and exposed ride across the flatter moor but the ascent is far from over. Ahead the road banks right and heads skyward, the dramatic finale to this long climb. The final testing, super-smooth section with a sheer drop to your right is marked 14% but seems harder as your legs scream from the effort to get up here. Roll round the left-hand bend to reach the barren windswept top.

FACTFILE

WHERE Leave the B6259 that travels through Nateby and turn onto the B6270 heading east. Pass through the village and begin to climb as you exit up the steep slope.

GRID REF NY 806 044 (OS91)

LENGTH 4050m

HEIGHT GAIN 302m

APPROX CLIMB TIME 17mins

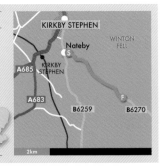

SLAIDBURN, LANCASHIRE

Perched at the highest point of the narrow road that links High Bentham with Slaidburn lies the stone that once held the ancient Cross of Greet. From either side there is plenty of climbing to be had but for the longest ascent, approach the summit from the Slaidburn side. Leaving the town, you'll have a couple of sizeable lumps to get over before dropping through a small wood to meet a stream. From here the road goes upwards to the summit. Bending slightly left, the early slopes are stiff but not too hard along the even but roughly-surfaced singletrack road. Enjoy the little depression before you cross the cattle grid, after which a number of mini peaks and troughs see your momentum ebb and flow. Now it's one step down and two steps up until you reach the deepest trough before the hardest part of the climb, a really stiff finale leading you round to the right to finish across a cattle grid high on top of the silent moor.

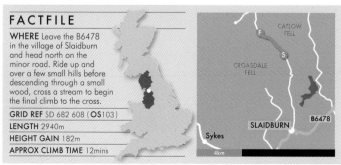

FACTFILE

WHERE Leave the B6478 in the village of Slaidburn and head north on the minor road. Ride up and over a few small hills before descending through a small wood, cross a stream to begin the final climb to the cross.

GRID REF SD 682 608 (**OS**103)	
LENGTH 2940m	
HEIGHT GAIN 182m	
APPROX CLIMB TIME 12mins	

80 HONISTER PASS

BUTTERMERE, CUMBRIA

The most beautiful of the Lake's passes, Honister offers a brilliant ride from either direction. Heading west from the village of Seatoller you face multiple sections of 25% gradient, however, the road rising from the valley heading eastwards will simply take your breath away. The towering sides of Buttermere Fell form a giant amphitheatre to ride through. Leaving Gatesgarth Farm the road climbs steadily for quite some time, passing over a small stone bridge, the real work begins as the rest of the road lies uncoiled before your eyes. Once past a jumble of huge slab-sided boulders you will cross a second stone bridge and onto a long, very testing 20% stretch leading to a mini plateau over the third and final bridge and onto vicious 25% slopes. Across the rough and rugged surface, you must eke your way through the imposing dark slate gates and on over the summit.

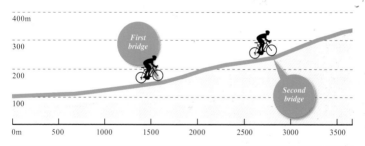

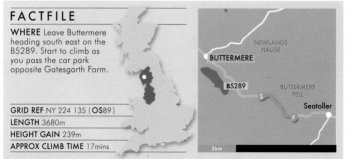

FACTFILE

WHERE Leave Buttermere heading south east on the B5289. Start to climb as you pass the car park opposite Gatesgarth Farm.

GRID REF NY 224 135 (**OS**89)

LENGTH 3680m

HEIGHT GAIN 239m

APPROX CLIMB TIME 17mins

81 NEWLANDS HAUSE

BUTTERMERE, CUMBRIA

Newlands Pass, rising up to Newlands Hause, links Buttermere in the west with Keswick in the east. The narrow road rises immediately at 20% from Buttermere then bends left and right, the rough bobbled road, very steep. Past a clump of trees, the gradient now eases as the landscape opens up, then there is a slight dip for a brief moment's rest before the hardest section. The road ahead bisects the epic grassy slope, climbing straight, long and very hard. With the green banking to the right and the abyss-like valley to the left the rider is dwarfed by the incredible scenery as the road rises to a right-hand bend. Round this and it's steeper again, the surface clean but still bumpy, the road narrowing further, eventually levelling for the briefest of moments, affording just enough time for you to size up the final 25% right-hard turn through rocks to the car park at the summit.

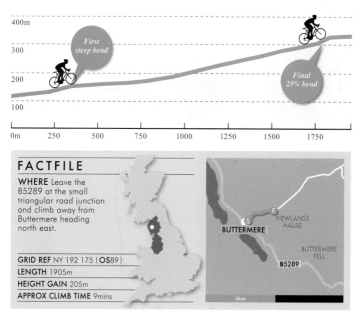

FACTFILE

WHERE Leave the B5289 at the small triangular road junction and climb away from Buttermere heading north east.

GRID REF NY 192 175 (OS89)

LENGTH 1905m

HEIGHT GAIN 205m

APPROX CLIMB TIME 9mins

BRAITHWAITE, CUMBRIA

Leaving the village of Braithwaite, just west of Keswick, the B5292 leads you over to Lorton Valley. Rough to start, this road follows a brook, kinks left then right into its steepest section, right at the start. Unlike the other major Cumbrian passes, Whinlattter is almost completely tree-lined as it doesn't reach the high altitudes of the others. After the rugged opening section the gradient eases and the surface improves as the climb begins snaking its way between the beautiful tall conifers. Once past a white cottage the road bends right, becoming steeper again, then left past a large car park before levelling out at Noble Knott and descending a little. Another section of climbing follows, then it's flat past Mass Mill before dipping once more before one final climb, a section of 15% to the park's visitors' centre. Short enough to attack with force, this last stretch finishes a beautiful climb of unique character in the UK.

FACTFILE

WHERE To climb Whinlatter Pass leave the village of Braithwaite heading west on the B5292 and climb into the forest.

GRID REF NY 206 244 (**OS89**)

LENGTH 3320m

HEIGHT GAIN 231m

APPROX CLIMB TIME 13mins

Thornthwaite
B5292
A591
A66
KESWICK
Braithwaite
DERWENT WATER
Little Town
B5289
4km

AMBLESIDE, CUMBRIA

The best way to tackle the A592 Kirkstone Pass is to attack it from the north. Take the road from the banks of Ullswater, through Bridgend to the base of the climb opposite the turning to Hartsop. A major route, though not too busy, its lower slopes are gentle as you follow the meandering path of Kirkstone Beck. Rounding a bend around two-thirds distance, the tarmac winds up steeply ahead of you, cutting its way between two rocky peaks. An excellent surface all the way up, the road is generally clean and smooth apart from a few repaired patches and grilles. The road never wavers far from its direct route to the top and once inside the final kilometre that's when things start to get serious. Reaching this short 20% section, the roadside is littered with giant cube-like boulders. Push on through here as it's only a brief struggle after which things get gradually easier as you approach the Kirkstone Passage Inn.

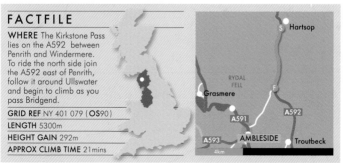

FACTFILE

WHERE The Kirkstone Pass lies on the A592 between Penrith and Windermere. To ride the north side join the A592 east of Penrith, follow it around Ullswater and begin to climb as you pass Bridgend.

GRID REF NY 401 079 (**OS**90)

LENGTH 5300m

HEIGHT GAIN 292m

APPROX CLIMB TIME 21mins

84 HARDKNOTT PASS

ESKDALE, CUMBRIA

The king of climbs and arguably the hardest road in the land, the legendary Hardknott Pass is an amazing sliver of tarmac. First built in 2AD by the Romans the pass is unbelievably tough from both directions. To climb from the east, begin at the warning sign at Jubilee Bridge. It's very steep into a small woodland, over a cattle grid and then you will see the enormity of your task. Yes, they did build a road over that! Enter the first of two sets of brutal switchbacks and wrench body and bike through the 25% corners. What follows is a brief levelling out but you can't put off what lies ahead for long. The second set of switchbacks are steeper still, and these now 30% slopes will have you straining every sinew as your front wheel desperately searches for a kinder gradient and weaves all over the road fighting to stay upright. If you can ride this, you can ride anything. Just keep going, then head down the terrifying descent.

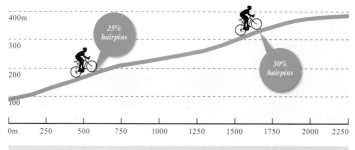

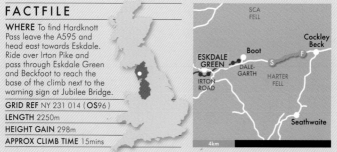

FACTFILE

WHERE To find Hardknott Pass leave the A595 and head east towards Eskdale. Ride over Irton Pike and pass through Eskdale Green and Beckfoot to reach the base of the climb next to the warning sign at Jubilee Bridge.

GRID REF NY 231 014 (**OS**96)

LENGTH 2250m

HEIGHT GAIN 298m

APPROX CLIMB TIME 15mins

east

If Hardknott is the king of climbs, then Wrynose is its queen; slightly softer at the edges but no less ruthless. The hardest ascent is from the west beginning at Fell Foot Farm, where straight away you have a 20% right-hander and that's just a taste of what lies ahead. The road levels slightly but the surface is cut up and damaged. Still, that's the least of your worries as you pass a 25% sign. A long long stretch of wickedly steep tarmac lies ahead, hugging the side of the mountain, with a slight levelling halfway but steeper still after that. Then you hit the switchbacks, where a better surface is cold comfort as you grapple with gravity's pull and attempt to hold your momentum through these vicious bends. Once through, you can pick up some speed before the final steep turns and your new found momentum will help carry you through these and over the top.

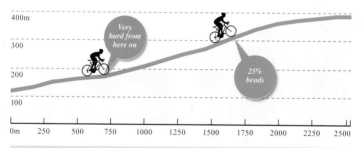

FACTFILE

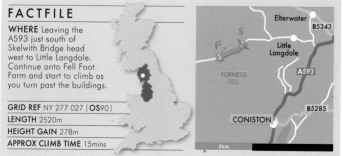

WHERE Leaving the A593 just south of Skelwith Bridge head west to Little Langdale. Continue onto Fell Foot Farm and start to climb as you turn past the buildings.

GRID REF NY 277 027 (OS90)

LENGTH 2520m

HEIGHT GAIN 278m

APPROX CLIMB TIME 15mins

WALES

91 Bwlch-y-Groes

89 The Road to Hell

87 Moel Arthur

92 Ffordd Penllech

88 Penbarra

93 Devil's Staircase

86 The Shelf

95 Black Mountain

90 Horseshoe Pass

ABERYSTWYTH

98 Rhigos

100 Constitution Hill

97 The Tumble

CARDIFF

96 Bryn Du

99 The Bwlch

94 Llangynidr Mountain

86 THE SHELF

RUTHIN, DENBIGHSHIRE

Ruthin is an excellent base to ride many climbs in north Wales and one such climb is The Shelf. Leave town heading south on the A525, take your first left, cross the B5429 then take a left and a right to find the base. The lower slopes are gentle and climb past numerous farm buildings and through many twists and turns. Away from the houses you see the landscape open up as you exit high towering hedgerows into a couple of steep switchbacks. The middle of this seemingly forgotten and gnarled stretch of road is gradually being reclaimed by nature, its broken surface pushed apart as grass and weeds force their way through the cracks to stake their claim. What little of the road you can find to ride on, now very narrow with thick gorse on your left and a steep drop on your right, eventually plateaus. Finally you turn round to the right and the end is in sight at the top of the brow.

FACTFILE

WHERE Leave Ruthin, heading south on the A525. Once out of town take your first left and cross to the B5429. Turn left at the junction then next right and immediate right again to begin the climb.

GRID REF SJ 172 536 (OS116)

LENGTH 5090m

HEIGHT GAIN 262m

APPROX CLIMB TIME 14mins

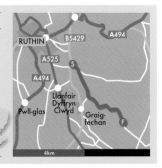

87 MOEL ARTHUR

LLANGWYFAN, DENBIGHSHIRE

Named after the remains of the Iron Age fort at its summit, this climb is toughest when tackled from the Denbigh side. Begin at the crossroads marked 'Groes-fawr'. You are soon dwarfed by immense, four-metre high hedgerows either side as you ascend the smooth narrow road. Getting steeper, with hardly enough room for a single vehicle, you leave the hedgerows and the road kinks right, steeper still, into a horrible little stretch. Bone-shakingly rough, lumpy, bumpy, broken and potholed, you bounce from ridge to crater, searching for traction as the road approaches 20%. Bending slightly left you are through the hardest part and the surface improves, but it's still uneven and you continue to skip around as the road weaves slightly left and right, climbing higher and higher. Finish the climb as you cross the cattle grid adjacent to the car park for the ancient fort.

FACTFILE

WHERE Travelling east from Denbigh cross the B5429 at Waen. Pass through the village, turn left to Llangwyfan then take a right. Once riding out of the village take the first left to begin the climb at Groes-fawr.

GRID REF SJ 146 657 (**OS**116)	
LENGTH 2245m	
HEIGHT GAIN 220m	
APPROX CLIMB TIME 11mins	

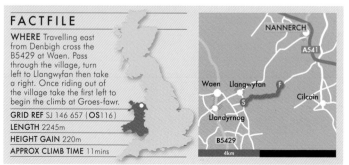

88 PENBARRA

LLANBEDR-DYFFRYN-CLWYD, DENBIGHSHIRE

Towering above Ruthin stands Bwlch Penbarra in the Moel Famau Park. Leave the
A494 east out of town and take the turn marked Lon Cae Glas. Rising steeply past
houses you have to contend with traffic calming obstacles every 100 metres or so
on the lower slopes. Reaching a T-junction, turn left and after a brief respite the road
ramps up hard, getting harder as it leaves the last of the houses behind, on a decent
surface heading dead straight. Crossing a cattle grid, the road climbs harder still as
it approaches a wicked but stunning left-hand bend. Framed by beautiful gorse, the
sweeping 25% corner is simply perfect, and as tough on the legs as it is easy on the
eyes. Exit, and the gradient shallows so you can reap the fruits of your labour in the
form of the dramatic view. Round to the right, past a clump of trees, the landscape
opens and the narrow road gets harder again as you grind your way to the finish.

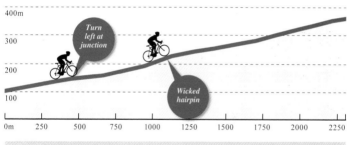

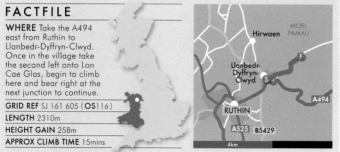

FACTFILE

WHERE Take the A494
east from Ruthin to
Llanbedr-Dyffryn-Clwyd.
Once in the village take
the second left onto Lon
Cae Glas, begin to climb
here and bear right at the
next junction to continue.

GRID REF SJ 161 605 (**OS**116)

LENGTH 2310m

HEIGHT GAIN 258m

APPROX CLIMB TIME 15mins

89 THE ROAD TO HELL

DENBIGH, DENBIGHSHIRE

This is a long climb by anyone's standards and will have you heading upwards for just over 11 kilometres. The road meanders out of Denbigh, then, from nowhere you hit a left-hand, 20% hairpin and the hurt begins. The smooth, wide road framed by tall hedges, eases, but the tranquillity doesn't last as the road soon starts to narrow, and as it narrows it steepens and its surface deteriorates. Ramping up, the climb kinks left past lunar-like craters, then sharp right and left again into a monstrously long 17% stretch, following which you are rewarded with a short, speedy descent. Still a long way from hell, keep right at a junction then enjoy the rolling contours for a while before you reach more serious climbing. Across a cattle grid the road enters epic open land as it follows the edge of the eerie Lake Brenig. Bending gently right, just one more strength-sapping push delivers you into the hands of the Devil.

FACTFILE

WHERE The B4501 starts from the centre of Denbigh. Leave the High Street and turn onto Lon Pendref, this turns into Love Lane. Travelling south follow the road west winding to the tight hairpin where you start.

GRID REF SH 970 581 (OS116)

LENGTH 11090m

HEIGHT GAIN 353m

APPROX CLIMB TIME 38mins

Bwlch yr Oernant, otherwise known as the Horseshoe Pass for its unique and dramatic topography, begins following a dip on the A542 from Pentrefelin. The sign says it's three miles to the summit and it's all uphill. The short steep beginning soon eases, then following the Abbey Grange Hotel it climbs steeper as it approaches Britannia Inn. The rough topping now climbs steeply into a short covering of trees, exits, then eases as it enters the 'horseshoe' and your ride up to its apex. A tight right, the sign reads 20% but that's an exaggeration – it's steep, but not that steep. Hug the left-hand side of the road, lined by a bank of scree. The road levels slightly then kicks hard right back out of the horseshoe. The exit route is gentle – look to your right for awesome views of the gorge below and follow the road round to the right to complete the climb adjacent to a large sign, proudly boasting the height of the pass.

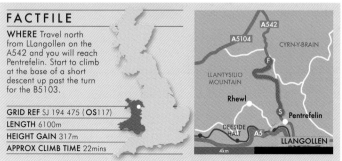

FACTFILE

WHERE Travel north from LLangollen on the A542 and you will reach Pentrefelin. Start to climb at the base of a short descent up past the turn for the B5103.

GRID REF SJ 194 475 (OS117)

LENGTH 6100m

HEIGHT GAIN 317m

APPROX CLIMB TIME 22mins

91 BWLCH-Y-GROES

DINAS MAWDDWY, GWYNEDD

Named Hellfire Pass by the English but better known by its Welsh name, Bwlch-y-Groes is the highest tarmacked pass in Wales. Climbing into the Aran Mountains on the edge of Snowdonia, its a road of outstanding beauty – rough, weathered and remorselessly steep. Leave the A470 at Dinas Mawddwy and head into the Afon Dyfi Valley. Once past an axle weight sign the climb begins. Passing farm buildings and trees, the road veers left then a very sharp 25% right – a taste of what's to come before easing as the last of the trees disappear beneath you. Now round to the right, the ever steepening, increasingly lumpy surface heads into arguably the hardest section of relentlessly steep tarmac in Britain. The sheer length of this steep section is what sets this climb apart, there's just nowhere to recover. You'll be counting each and every pedal rev as you slowly push your way up the scree-littered road to the summit.

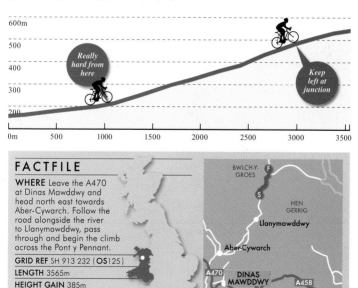

FACTFILE

WHERE Leave the A470 at Dinas Mawddwy and head north east towards Aber-Cywarch. Follow the road alongside the river to Llanymawddwy, pass through and begin the climb across the Pont y Pennant.

GRID REF SH 913 232 (OS125)

LENGTH 3565m

HEIGHT GAIN 385m

APPROX CLIMB TIME 23mins

92 FFORDD PENLLECH

HARLECH, GWYNEDD

Forget Rosedale, forget Hardknott – Ffordd Penllech is the steepest hill in the land. Tucked away in Harlech behind the Castle lies a tiny road that has to be seen to be believed. Unfortunately it's a one-way street and you need to ride it against the flow, but those mad enough to try will face very little traffic as it's a nerve-shredding descent in any vehicle. Leave the A496, turning right just before a level crossing, then right again past a caravan park, then kiss your saddle goodbye as you'll not be able to sit down until the finish. The first ridiculous bend is in front of you, the tarmac ripped and scarred as if it's been attacked by some prehistoric creature – in reality the undersides of vehicles. If you can round this 40% bend it continues crazy steep all the way up, kinking left and right and passing by houses. At its easiest it's never less than 20%. By the time you reach the tourist shops at the top you'll be ready to collapse.

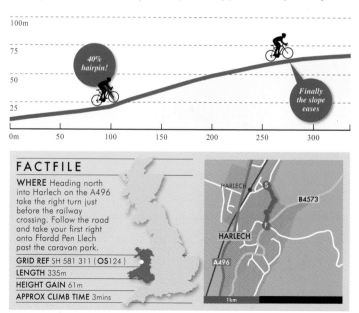

FACTFILE

WHERE Heading north into Harlech on the A496 take the right turn just before the railway crossing. Follow the road and take your first right onto Ffordd Pen Llech past the caravan park.

GRID REF SH 581 311 (OS124)

LENGTH 335m

HEIGHT GAIN 61m

APPROX CLIMB TIME 3mins

ABERGWESYN, POWYS

Deep in the Welsh wilderness, far from civilization, lies a hill that needs little introduction. There seems little reason to build a road out here, never mind one this steep. But here it is: The Devil's Staircase. Leave the village of Abergwesyn and climb gently through the isolation to a couple of bridges in the rocky valley and you're at base camp. The road disappears into the trees ahead, with a weathered sign warning you of the gradient you face. Straight away the very narrow, rough surface ramps up to 25%. Grind your way up into the eerie conifers to reach a hairpin left-hander. The road levels a little round the bend, allowing you to catch your breath, but then you are straight into the next incredibly tough stretch to a sharp, very steep right-hander, un-rideable at its apex. The surface on the high slopes is good and after the second hard turn it eases but still climbs hard for quite some time before you reach the top.

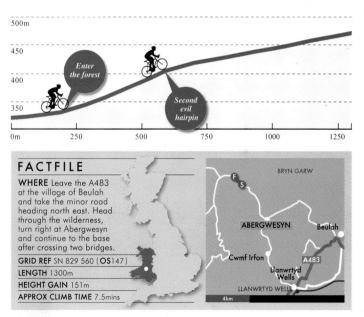

FACTFILE

WHERE Leave the A483 at the village of Beulah and take the minor road heading north east. Head through the wilderness, turn right at Abergwesyn and continue to the base after crossing two bridges.

GRID REF SN 829 560 (OS147)

LENGTH 1300m

HEIGHT GAIN 151m

APPROX CLIMB TIME 7.5mins

RATING

7/10

94 LLANGYNIDR MOUNTAIN

LLANGYNIDR, POWYS

The base to this monster climb can be found just east of Llangynidr. Leave the B4558 onto the B4560 and begin your ascent up the smooth and gentle early slopes. Make the most of this warm-up past farmhouses and through woodland as you continue climbing round to the right. Bending past a white cottage on the left, the road climbs steeply into a left-hand hairpin. Over the cattle grid, the road narrowing, you switch back on yourself and head up to a sweeping right-hander. It's wild up here on the best of days, but if the weather turns it can be a very inhospitable place. Pass a car park and you may think you're at the top, but no – over the brow you see there's more climbing to be done. Down the dip, sweep round the fast left-hand bend before your legs scream as you climb once more up a short nasty grind veering right and finally to the mountain summit.

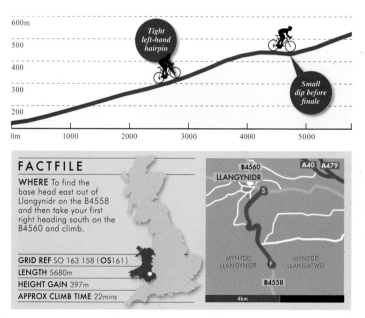

FACTFILE

WHERE To find the base head east out of Llangynidr on the B4558 and then take your first right heading south on the B4560 and climb.

GRID REF SO 163 158 (**OS**161)

LENGTH 5680m

HEIGHT GAIN 397m

APPROX CLIMB TIME 22mins

95 BLACK MOUNTAIN

LLANGADOG, CARMARTHENSHIRE

Not to be confused with the Black Mountains, the Black Mountain range is the furthest west of the Brecon Beacons. For the toughest ascent take the A4069 south from Llangadog and begin to climb as you pass through the small village of Pont Aber. It starts gently, gradient twisting through trees and past farmhouses, the wide, well marked and well surfaced road heading onwards and upwards. After a long slog you reach a cattle grid and from here the scenery changes, now rugged, exposed and wild. The gradient is still gentle though, until you reach a hairpin across an old stone bridge, from where it climbs steeper. The road, a little damaged in the gutter, bends left then right and through a wonderful snaking S-bend framed by two trees. Continue up to a left-hand hairpin and into the final stretch, bending right onto the windswept open summit next to a car park on your right.

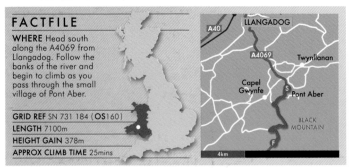

FACTFILE

WHERE Head south along the A4069 from Llangadog. Follow the banks of the river and begin to climb as you pass through the small village of Pont Aber.

GRID REF SN 731 184 (**OS**160)

LENGTH 7100m

HEIGHT GAIN 378m

APPROX CLIMB TIME 25mins

96 BRYN DU

ABERDARE, RHONDDA CYNON TAFF

Climbing from the centre of Aberdare, this mountain road has a glorious collection of twists and turns at the top. It's very steep straight away as you weave out of the valley. Initially a shock to the system, the early part of this climb can be split into two sections, the first hard, the second harder then bearing right. Crossing the ubiquitous cattle grid, marking your exit from civilization and your entry to the wilderness, the surface turns silky smooth and climbs steeply to the first of four hairpins. First turning left, the gradient shallow round the corner then steep into a long straight to the second, a perfectly engineered right-hander allowing you to sweep round with no need for extra effort or change of gear. Flow on towards the third. Steeper still you bank left then right soon after. Once through these exhilarating bends you are left with the long gentle stretch until the road dips over the other side.

FACTFILE

WHERE To start the climb leave Victoria Square in the centre of Aberdare heading south west on the A4233, Monk Street.

GRID REF SS 972 997 (OS170)
LENGTH 5575m
HEIGHT GAIN 270m
APPROX CLIMB TIME 13.5mins

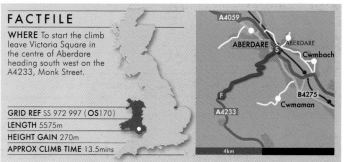

97 THE TUMBLE

GOVILON, MONMOUTHSHIRE

One of the most feared and frequently raced climbs in Wales, The Tumble offers an excellent challenge to any rider. Begin the climb as the B4246 leaves the village of Govilon and enters the Blaenavon World Heritage Site. Climb gently past houses and the little kick over the bridge then bend hard left where the road becomes steeper through the trees. Next, bending sharp right, the tarmac deteriorates as you begin the long abrasive slog, in and out from under the cover of the trees and all very hard going. Things get smoother once over the cattle grid though the gradient assures a uniformly strength-sapping ascent to slowly and surely wear the rider down. Approaching the upper section there looms dark, almost otherworldly rock formations to the right, creating an eerie, cool microclimate around the summit. Pass Keepers Pond on the right and finish just past a junction on the left.

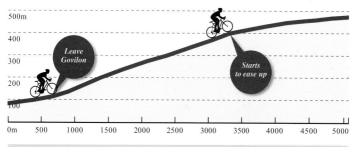

FACTFILE

WHERE Begin to climb the B4246 at the T-junction just south of and parallel to the A465. Enter Govilon and continue to ride through the village, out and upwards.

GRID REF SO 254 106 (**OS**161)

LENGTH 5100m

HEIGHT GAIN 399m

APPROX CLIMB TIME 22mins

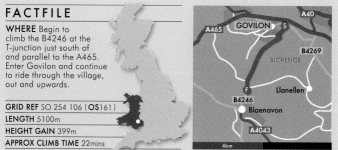

98 RHIGOS

HIRWAUN, RHONDDA CYNON TAFF

Start your ascent from the Hirwaun Industrial Estate to begin the dead straight, featureless slog up onto Hirwaun Common. The road is hard, but not too steep – a solid grind, bending left past the old Tower Colliery, the good road surface punctuated by large raised iron grilles in the gutter. Round the bend the gradient increases as you enter another long straight before turning right into a conifer plantation where you're treated to a couple of Alpine-style hairpins. Here you can see the road towering above on the left as you head to a smooth tight bend. Shallowing slightly before the turn but climbing steeper out of it, the climb goes hard up the side of the mountain with a substantial barrier on the left and a sheer rock face to the right. Now sweeping round to the right, the surface is rough and broken. Push yourself through this hostile territory to finish over the brow past a car park on the right.

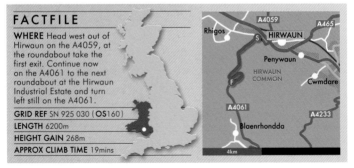

FACTFILE

WHERE Head west out of Hirwaun on the A4059, at the roundabout take the first exit. Continue now on the A4061 to the next roundabout at the Hirwaun Industrial Estate and turn left still on the A4061.

GRID REF SN 925 030 (**OS**160)

LENGTH 6200m

HEIGHT GAIN 268m

APPROX CLIMB TIME 19mins

     WALES

99 THE BWLCH

Most hills have two routes to the top but few can boast three almost equally challenging accents. The Bwlch can be attacked from either Treorchy, Price Town or, for the longest accent, from Cymer. To climb from Price Town, head north, climbing steeply away from the dilapidated clock tower up to a tough left-hand turn. The road flattens past houses on your right, dips then rises again very gently away from the village, across a cattle grid and into the forest. After a few twists and turns the road meanders left to lead into a sweeping right-hand hairpin nestled in a green, rocky bowl. Climbing hard, the perfectly smooth road rises in the shadow of the mountain, its jagged face held back by a solid stone wall. Over the brow, turn left and dip down to the junction with the A4107. Turn right towards Cymer and continue to climb round to the right until you finally reach the summit and you drop down to ride another route up.

FACTFILE

WHERE Enter Price Town on the A4061, at the roundabout take the second exit and begin to climb on the A4061. To get to the summit turn onto the A4107 at the junction of the three routes and continue.

GRID REF	SS 920 951 (**OS**170)
LENGTH	5790m
HEIGHT GAIN	340m
APPROX CLIMB TIME	21mins

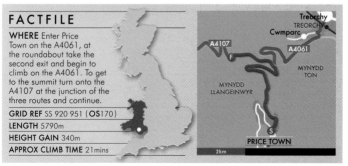

100 CONSTITUTION HILL

SWANSEA

Hidden in the heart of Swansea lies the infamous Constitution Hill, an excellently preserved and immaculately maintained cobbled climb just waiting to give you hell. The legality of climbing the hill may be questioned – no entry signs at the bottom and bollards preventing entry at the top suggest you shouldn't, but it's an essential climb for all cyclists to conquer. Begin at the junction with Hanover Street, ignore the signs, take whatever run up you can get and hit its wickedly steep gradient. The cobbles are large, even and framed either side by two feet of smooth paving which is far easier to ride. You've not truly ridden this hill if you haven't subjected your body to the pounding and jarring of the cobbles though. Heave and haul your machine past the various roads that intersect from both sides to finish, shaken and stirred, through the bollards at Terrace Road.

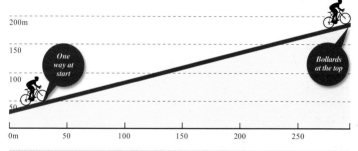

One way at start

Bollards at the top

200m

150

100

50

0m   50   100   150   200   250

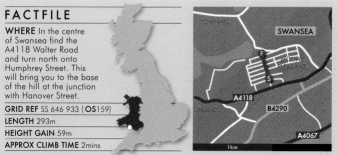

FACTFILE

WHERE In the centre of Swansea find the A4118 Walter Road and turn north onto Humphrey Street. This will bring you to the base of the hill at the junction with Hanover Street.

GRID REF SS 646 933 (**OS**159)

LENGTH 293m

HEIGHT GAIN 59m

APPROX CLIMB TIME 2mins

CONQUER THEM ALL

Your challenge, should you decide to accept it, is to ride these 100 climbs. Provided here, is a handy check list for you to log your times and chart your progress. So get out your maps, work the hills into your routes then head out to race, or maybe push your friends to the top of all these iconic roads. Good luck.

No	Hill	Date Ridden	Time
	SOUTH-WEST		
1	Cheddar Gorge		
2	Weston Hill		
3	Crowcombe Combe		
4	Porlock		
5	Dunkery Beacon		
6	Exmoor Forest		
7	Challacombe		
8	Dartmeet		
9	Haytor Vale		
10	Widecombe		
11	Rundlestone		
12	Salcombe Hill		
13	Dover's Hill		

No	Hill	Date Ridden	Time
	SOUTH-EAST		
14	Box Hill		
15	York's Hill		
16	White Lane		
17	Leith Hill		
18	White Downs		
19	The Wall		
20	Toys Hill		
21	Steyning Bostal		

No	Hill	Date Ridden	Time
22	Ditchling Beacon		
23	Whiteleaf		
24	Streatley Hill		
25	Combe Gibbet		
26	Mott Street		
27	Swains Lane		

MIDLANDS

No	Hill	Date Ridden	Time
28	Michaelgate		
29	Terrace Hill		
30	Monsal Head		
31	Bank Road		
32	Riber		
33	Winnats Pass		
34	Rowsley Bar		
35	Curbar Edge		
36	Mow Cop		
37	Peaslows		
38	Jiggers Bank		
39	The Burway		

YORKSHIRE

No	Hill	Date Ridden	Time
40	Shibden Wall		
41	Pea Royd Lane		
42	Jackson Bridge		
43	Holme Moss		
44	Halifax Lane		
45	Park Rash		
46	Oxnop Scar		
47	Malham Cove		
48	Langcliffe Scar		

No	Hill		
49	Buttertubs Pass		
50	Fleet Moss		
51	Tan Hill		
52	Greenhow Hill		
53	Norwood Edge		
54	Boltby Bank		
55	Rosedale Chimney		
56	White Horse Bank		
57	The Stang		
58	Carlton Bank		

NORTH-EAST

No	Hill	Date Ridden	Time
59	Crawleyside		
60	Peth Bank		
61	Winters Gibbet		
62	Chapel Fell		

SCOTLAND

No	Hill	Date Ridden	Time
63	Mennock Pass		
64	Cairn O' Mount		
65	The Cairnwell		
66	The Lecht		
67	Cairn Gorm		
68	Rest and be Thankful		
69	Bealach-na-Ba		

NORTH-WEST

No	Hill	Date Ridden	Time
70	Cat and Fiddle		
71	Swiss Hill		
72	The Rake		

CHECKLIST

No	Hill	Date Ridden	Time
73	Garsdale Head		
74	Nick of Pendle		
75	Trough of Bowland		
76	Jubilee Tower		
77	Hartside		
78	Lamps Moss		
79	Cross of Greet		
80	Honister Pass		
81	Newlands Hause		
82	Whinlatter Pass		
83	Kirkstone Pass		
84	Hardknott Pass		
85	Wrynose Pass		

WALES			
No	Hill	Date Ridden	Time
86	The Shelf		
87	Moel Arthur		
88	Penbarra		
89	The Road to Hell		
90	Horseshoe Pass		
91	Bwlch-y-Groes		
92	Ffordd Penllech		
93	Devil's Staircase		
94	Llangynidr Mountain		
95	Black Mountain		
96	Bryn Du		
97	The Tumble		
98	Rhigos		
99	The Bwlch		
100	Constitution Hill		

THANK YOU

I'd like to thank all the people who've inspired me to make this book and thank those who've very generously helped me make it. Firstly, thank you to the unwavering support, love and encouragement of my parents. Thank you to my wife Charlotte and daughter Lux for putting up with this project and enduring a few quite unique holidays as I rode up hill after hill. To my sister Clara and her husband Brian for giving up hours of their time cross checking my facts and following me around their adopted Yorkshire Dales. Next I'd like to thank Simon Hursthouse for his amazing generosity in giving his time to help me get my text up to scratch, I would not have had the confidence to complete the project without your help.

Thanks to Luke Evans for giving me the push I needed to get the project going and to Nick Burton for his companionship and suffering on many epic rides. Thanks to Gordon Kanki-Knight for listening to my ideas, checking text and giving me crucial advice when I needed it and thanks to all at Frances Lincoln for making the dream a reality.

Of the people who've inspired me since I started cycling I'd like to thank my uncle David for introducing me to bike racing and all those in the early days at Newark Castle CC. Thank you to all my cycling companions past and present, especially, Chris Moores, Mike Moss, Richard Hallet, and all at Norwood Paragon CC and Herne Hill velodrome.

To my heroes, Greg LeMond, and Graham Obree, the latter who has inspired my life so much, not just on the bike.

Finally to all others I drew inspiration from, and received help from along the way. To Simon Richardson, Paul and Suzy Moffat, Andy Waterman, Paul McGuigan, Jason Humphries, Richard Horne, Lionel Birnie, *Cycling Weekly*, Andy Jones, Jan and Carl Smyth and Dr Maciej Mazurek. And the man who lent me a tool to fix my chain in the freezing rain at the top of Halifax Lane. Thank you.

THE END